Praise for *Autopilot*

Too many great educators are burning out because the job is running them, not the other way around. *Autopilot* is the road map to take school leaders from surviving to thriving. It provides the tools to clear the clutter, calm the chaos, and rediscover the joy and purpose that brought us into leadership in the first place.

—**Tony Cattani,** proud principal of Lenape High School and 2025 NASSP Secondary Principal of the Year

School leadership has never been more complex, and that's why Rich Czyz's practical wisdom has never been more needed. Czyz has an established reputation for transforming overwhelming challenges into actionable solutions, and this latest gift delivers what so many need right now: a way out of the chaos. *Autopilot* isn't about doing more—it's about doing what matters most without completely burning out in the process. In an era when school leaders are drowning in demands from every direction, this book throws the life preserver.

—**Angela Stockman,** author of *The Writing Teacher's Guide to Pedagogical Documentation: Rethinking How We Assess Learners and Learning*

Autopilot is a must-read for anyone navigating the fast-paced, often overwhelming world of school leadership. With the seasoned insight of an educator who has been in the trenches, Czyz identifies the everyday pitfalls of inefficiency, distraction, and burnout—and offers clear, actionable strategies to overcome them. Acting as your trusted captain, he charts a steady course toward focus, efficiency, and peak performance. This is more than a guidebook; it's a lifeline for leaders who want to thrive, not just survive, in today's schools.

—**Amy Storer,** instructional coach and tech integration mentor

If you've ever led a school, you know the grind: constant demands, endless email, and barely any time for the vision that called you to the role in the first place. In *Autopilot*, Rich Czyz hands school leaders a smart, usable system for getting out of reactive mode and into high-impact leadership. A great read for anyone in the principal's chair.

—**Dr. Kara Stern,** director of education at SchoolStatus

Your school's rhythm starts with you. If you're stressed and stuck, that's the track your community will keep spinning. *Autopilot* flips the script. This book is the ultimate tool kit for cutting through the static so you can amplify your signal, reclaim your time, and lead with clarity and heart. Every great mixtape has flow, and this one gives you the high-impact moves to energize your staff, celebrate your students, and keep your culture thriving. Drop the needle on this one—it's essential listening for every principal ready to make their mark.

—**Sean Gaillard,** principal and author

A great school culture doesn't just happen, and it's very hard to build when you are stuck in email and paperwork. *Autopilot* takes care of the nuts and bolts—the systems and schedules—so leaders can step out of the weeds and put their energy where it matters most: building a strong, positive culture and providing instructional leadership necessary for schools to grow.

—**Jay Billy,** proud principal of Bear Tavern Elementary School and author of *Lead with Culture*

Rich Czyz delivers exactly what every school leader needs but rarely has time to seek out: practical, tested strategies that cut through the noise and create space for meaningful work. With candor, clarity, and a deep understanding of the unique challenges in education, Rich offers a flight plan that doesn't just make you more efficient—it helps you lead with focus, intention, and impact.

—**Mike Vardy,** productivity strategist and author of *The Productivity Diet*

AUTOPILOT

AUTOPILOT

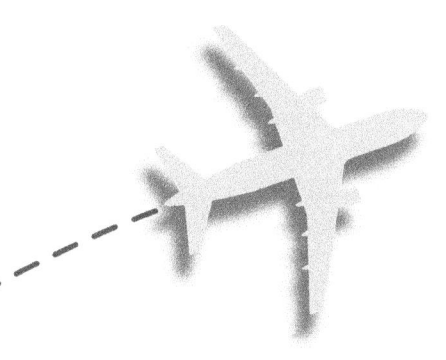

PRACTICAL
PRODUCTIVITY
FOR
SCHOOL LEADERS

RICH CZYZ

Autopilot: Practical Productivity for School Leaders
© 2025 Rich Czyz

All rights reserved. No part of this publication may be reproduced in any form or by any electronic or mechanical means, including information storage and retrieval systems, without permission in writing by the publisher, except by a reviewer who may quote brief passages in a review. For information regarding permission, contact the publisher at books@daveburgessconsulting.com.

This book is available at special discounts when purchased in quantity for educational purposes or for use as premiums, promotions, or fundraisers. For inquiries and details, contact the publisher at books@daveburgessconsulting.com.

Published by Dave Burgess Consulting, Inc.
Vancouver, WA
DaveBurgessConsulting.com

Library of Congress Control Number: 2025944205
Paperback ISBN: 978-1-968898-06-9
Ebook ISBN: 978-1-968898-02-1

Cover and interior design by Liz Schreiter
Edited and produced by Reading List Editorial
ReadingListEditorial.com

Megan, thank you for your never-ending love, encouragement, and support.

Meredith, thank you for your love and support, for being my first editor and talking through the book during our road trip.

Olivia and Malcolm, thank you for your love and support, and for always listening to productivity podcasts in the car even when I know you really don't want to.

CONTENTS

1: Welcome Aboard! 1
2: Your Captain 4
3: Defining Autopilot 6
4: The Path Forward and the Preflight Checklist 11

The Autopilot Strategies

5: Start with the Basics: Email Solutions and Communication
   Overload 16
     To Email, or Not to Email, That Is the Question 17
     Inbox Zero 18
     Email Templates and Premail 18
     Control Panel Check: Schedule Emails 21
     Avoid Email Tag 22
     Get a Bigger BOAT! 25
     Organize Your Inbox 28
     Control Panel Check: FAQs 29
     Find Me a Find, Batch Me a Batch 30

6: Mastering Your Time and Energy 34
     Eat a Frog (or a Bigger Frog) 34
     The Two-Minute Rule 35
     The Touch-It-Once Rule 35
     Control Panel Check: Self-Emails 36
     Bento Box Productivity 37
     The Power of Breaks 38
     Control Panel Check: Calendar Reminders to Get Out and About . . . 40
     Leave Space in the Margin 40
     Take Advantage of Early and Late Hours 43
     Use Your Time Wisely—Schedule Office Hours 43
     My Dream Schedule 47
     Theme Days 49
     Having Nothing Planned (or Planning to Do Nothing) 52

7: Conquering Procrastination and Perfectionism 54
- Productivity, Motivation, and Procrastination 54
- Other Methods for Managing Procrastination 57
- Overcoming Perfectionism 58
- Trade-Offs 61
- Give Yourself Over to the Idea of Tomorrow 62
- What to Do When the Internet Doesn't Work 63
- The Single Most Important Piece of Technology That We Own 64
- Why You Need a Phone Jail 65

8: Automation, Delegation, and Empowerment 67
- Multitasking Versus Multi-Asking 67
- Delegate and Elevate 69
- Customer Support Tickets 70
- Your Problem or Theirs? 71
- Control Panel Check: Autosave Attachments 75
- Dealing with Staff Absences 75
- Dealing with Discipline 79
- Automated Walk-Through Feedback 82
- Who's the Instructional Leader, Anyway? 84
- Control Panel Check: Auto Tabs 88

9: Streamlining Your Workflows 89
- Your Old Friend, Elimination 89
- Eliminate Decisions 91
- The Checklist Mentality 93
- The Notebook 94
- The URGENT Umbrella 97
- Funnel Forward 99
- How to Organize Folders 102
- Control Panel Check: A Family Folder 104
- Plug and Play—Why Scripts Are the Solution You Didn't Know You Needed 104

10: Creating a Focused, Productive Environment 107
- Avoid Your To-Do List. Try a To-Don't List Instead. 107
- Creating a Culture of School Productivity 109
- Create a Distraction List 111
- Parade Through the Rain 112
- Celebrate Productivity Wins 114

    Airplane Mode and Cave Time 115
    The Importance of the Office 117
    Control Panel Check: Desktop Organizer 121

11: Routines and Rituals for Success 123
    No-Office Days and No-Distraction Days 123
    Schedule Your Decisions 125
    End-of-Day Shutdown Rituals and Routines 128
    Control Panel Check: Read Later 130
    The Seven Stages of Sunday Night 130
    The Importance of Summer 134
    The Quicker Picker Upper 135
    Travel Size (or a Trial Period) 137
    The Best Twenty Dollars I Ever Spent 139
    Control Panel Check: Reminder Emails 140

12: Our Final Approach 141

13: Designing Your FLIGHT Plan 144

14: Earn Your Productivity Wings 149

15: A Final Message from Our Captain 151

Beyond Autopilot 152

Acknowledgments 153

About Rich Czyz 154

More from Dave Burgess Consulting, Inc. 155

WELCOME ABOARD!

If you've been a school leader, you know.
If you just became a school leader, congratulations. You'll soon find out.

It's never been harder to be an administrator than it is right now.

I assumed that after several years in different school administrative roles, the job would become easier. I couldn't have been more wrong.

Each day, jobs in school administration become increasingly complex, with unimagined challenges, disastrous surprises, and numerous roadblocks appearing at your door. We all sometimes struggle with inefficiency, idleness, and a lack of focus.

The fire alarm goes off unexpectedly because it was pulled by a high school (or preschool!) student. You need to send a letter to parents announcing a staff resignation. Five students end up in the office from two separate incidents when you are scheduled to meet with a teacher for a postobservation conference. The superintendent calls to say that a parent complained to a school board member about the lack of a crossing guard during morning arrival. Amid all of this, you are trying to be present with students and teachers in the classroom. When 3:15 p.m. rolls around, you finally start writing up the agenda for the staff meeting that starts in twenty minutes.

No one ever said it was going to be easy, but no one explained that it would be this hard. As I often say to those around me when something unexpected happens, they certainly didn't teach me this in principal school. No one is fully prepared to be a school leader, and no one has all of the answers. Even the best school leaders go through rough patches and unexpected surprises before somehow coming out on the other end in one piece. Sometimes, it's simply about survival. And sometimes, it's more about preparation than anything else.

You have to find a way to run the school before the school runs you.

Let's take a moment to understand the reasons behind our inefficiency and struggles. Being a school leader can be downright overwhelming most of the time. Your plate is full. You are constantly filling the plates of others, and more gets added on a regular basis. The workload you currently face isn't getting any smaller. In fact, a majority of the work you commit to each day probably seems like busywork—pointless, time-consuming administrative tasks that take you away from the work you were meant to do: supporting students and teachers. Unfortunately, most of your time is dedicated to duties that keep you far away from the classroom.

How much work do you take home each night? How much time do you spend checking and answering emails after hours? Too much. You're swamped. You want to finish everything during the school day but can't. If you could just reduce your workload, you might actually feel better about leaving your work at work. Unfortunately, it can feel as if the pile of stuff is never ending. We reinvent from year to year and constantly face the latest and greatest new initiatives driven by decision-makers who have never seen the inside of a school. The hits just keep on coming. (And they don't stop coming—thank you, Smash Mouth!)

Let's face it. Our jobs are hard. They can cause stress that we don't always deal with in the healthiest of ways. I know that my workload in school has sometimes negatively impacted my relationships at work *and* at home. The busyness that we cling to serves as a badge of honor.

We proudly proclaim that we are "slammed at work" or "busy beyond belief." All this "pride" does, though, is form a shield around the minutiae that take our days from us. We keep going because it's the only way we know how. It doesn't need to be this way.

How can anyone perform this job at the highest level? There is a way. We are all looking for a new approach. Going on autopilot can help to alleviate some of the pressure and anxiety and allow us to feel a sense of accomplishment for the impactful work we're doing. This book is going to get you flying toward improved efficiency and increased productivity—finally. And it's about damn time.

> *Attention all school leaders. This is your captain speaking.*
>
> *We are cleared for departure to our incredible destination of unparalleled productivity. We will ascend to new heights of efficiency and are set to achieve peak performance. Secure your belongings, adjust your seats to the upright position, and prepare for takeoff.*
>
> *Welcome aboard.*

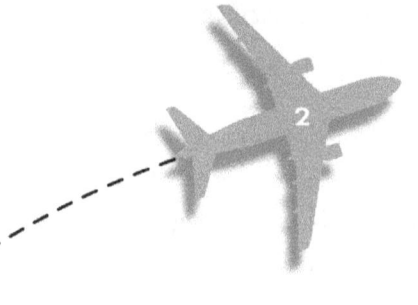

YOUR CAPTAIN

I'll be your captain as we head toward our final destination. I will share my experience to help you become a more productive school leader. I've previously served as a supervisor, a central office director, and a technology and curriculum coach. I currently work as a school principal. I have served as an administrator for nearly fifteen of my twenty years as an educator. In that time, I've figured out a few things. I'm going to be completely honest and tell you that I don't have all the answers—but I can share some solutions that will make you more efficient in the following areas:

- streamlined communication
- time management and scheduling
- organization and planning
- collaboration and delegation
- decision-making and prioritization

I've spent my career seeking out the best ways to do things. I don't always figure it out on the first try, but most of my successes have happened because I was always willing to experiment. Curiosity has led me to try different approaches—some that worked and some that didn't. I want to share the strategies, systems, and methods that I've developed and learned from others. These approaches help me to not only stay on the correct flight path but also keep ahead in a world where you can very quickly run into turbulence.

Educational leadership can be a very lonely place. You may be the sole administrator in your school, like I am. Or you may have another school leader or two who you are working with. You may be the only curriculum supervisor serving five schools, or you may be working along with one other person to serve seventeen schools. You may be an instructional coach, a team leader, a teacher leader, or a head of a department. It doesn't matter what leadership role you hold. You may not even hold an official title but still serve as a leader among your colleagues. Regardless of your title, there's a ton of work. I know you are asked to complete ten thousand tasks while balancing another hundred and, at the same time, putting out several fires. Your to-do list constantly grows no matter how many items you check off. Each day's battles are numerous, and you fight valiantly to feel accomplished. School leadership can be a very lonely place, and very quiet. I get it. But it doesn't have to be that way. It's time that you figured out how to switch to autopilot. It's time for you to set your flight path, check all systems, and discover your true north for practical productivity.

As we prepare to learn more about what I mean by *autopilot*, I want to share a personal anecdote about my first job as an administrator. I was hired as an elementary supervisor to work with teachers in four different buildings. My first office was a converted classroom that sat in the middle of a pod of second- and third-grade classrooms. The office, known as the "fishbowl," had windows on all sides and, with the shades pulled up, I could be seen by all of the surrounding classrooms, students and teachers alike. As a brand-new administrator, the fishbowl only heightened my awareness that everyone was watching. As I've continued in my role as a school leader, I've taken that experience in the fishbowl and tried to bring transparency to everything that I do. Now, I want you to peer into the fishbowl and find the productivity systems and strategies that can help you too.

DEFINING AUTOPILOT

Now, I know exactly what you're thinking. You want to immediately reach maximum productivity in your work. Luckily, I'm here to help you discover the strategies and systems that can lead you to that destination. Before we get to all that, let's clearly define what we mean by *autopilot*:

> Autopilot enables school leaders to be more effective through the adoption of automated systems, organized processes, and strategic productivity techniques. These systems and techniques ultimately allow school leaders to navigate their complex roles with increased focus, efficiency, and impact.

You will ultimately need to discover which systems, processes, and techniques work for you. The ideas and strategies in this book are not intended as the be-all and end-all solution to your productivity and automation needs. The beautiful part of all of this is that you can experiment. You can try a strategy, remix it, and make it work for you.

If you walk away with just one idea that helps you to be more productive, then I will consider the book a major success.

I define *productivity* as the ability to work efficiently, effectively, and sustainably to accomplish the meaningful work of a school leader.

The key word in this definition is *meaningful*. Productivity for school administrators is not simply getting the busywork done. It's also about the meaningful work we do every day: helping teachers move forward with their instruction, connecting with students and families, and ensuring that students walk out of the building as better people than they were when they walked in.

Being productive also means tackling the busywork and administrivia with a certain efficiency so you have time for the important stuff. It means being effective in how you accomplish things and, more importantly, sustaining efficiency over time. We don't want school leaders to continue to flame out because there is simply too much on their plates. Autopilot strategies should help you to be more efficient and effective while also managing to sustain your efforts without burning out.

A WORD ABOUT BURNOUT

In recent years, education has seen a significant shift. We have learned more about mental health, and we've seen educators decide that they are going to try to strike a better work-life balance. We've also seen educators who are burned out and leaving the profession.

This book includes strategies to ensure that you will not burn out. Yes, you will find actions that will help you streamline your day, but you'll also find ways to stop for a moment and catch your breath. Going on autopilot is not about clearing more time in your day so that you can go 120 miles per hour instead of your normal 90. It's really about

> making room for the meaningful, and doing so in a healthy and safe manner.
>
> All of us have the ability to be better at what we do and to avoid taking on so much that it pushes us to the brink of our profession. While you are employing some of the strategies that help you to be more efficient, make sure you are employing the strategies that also help you to take a breath.

Now let's tackle another important term. We usually think of automation as involving some sort of machine taking over a human task. Think of the automated phone systems that drive all of us crazy (why can't somebody just answer the phone?). Automation typically uses some type of technology to streamline a process. But I want to add a key caveat to that definition for the purposes of autopilot:

> *Automation* is defined as any task or process that we can perform automatically through the use of technology and/or human help.

That's right: In schools, automation can also involve human help. Let's give an example. At our school, fifth-grade students handle the morning announcements. We've developed a streamlined process in which students use a template to create and deliver the announcements each day. I train a team of four to five students for about two weeks at the start of the year, ensuring they can independently manage the entire process. After that initial training, any team member can perform any task, and the system runs smoothly year after year. This meets our definition of automation, because it's simplifying a task that might normally fall on the school leader. Instead, the task is completed automatically, with human help—our awesome fifth-grade announcements team.

Let's examine one more important term that will help us as we move through the book.

Pain points are the persistent or recurring parts of your day that frequently inconvenience, annoy, or stop you from accomplishing your most meaningful work.

Going on autopilot is easier said than done. We've already talked about the complexity of the job. School leadership is increasingly difficult in an increasingly changing world. You know how overwhelming the job can be: the mental demands, the time constraints, the being pulled in six directions at once, and, most importantly, the emotional fatigue that comes with making decisions in the best interests of everyone around you.

What keeps you from doing your best and most productive work? There are probably many contributing factors to your struggles. As you read through this book, you should be able to identify your pain points and find strategies to replace them with more productive habits.

Consider these questions as you think about your school day:

- Do you spend all day tackling your inbox and answering emails, only to find your inbox full again by the end of the day?
- Do you have a never-ending list of administrative tasks that take up most of your day?
- Do you feel like your to-do list is really just a list of other people's to-do items?
- Do you not have enough time in your day to visit with students and teachers?
- Do you spend your entire day putting out fires—unexpected occurrences that swallow your time wholesale?
- Do you struggle to finish your daily goals?
- Do you push off work until the next day?
- Do you stay late to finish your work?
- Do you struggle to streamline your work?

If you answered yes to any of these questions, then the pages that follow are going to be crucial. The pages that follow are going to allow you to eliminate some of your pain points. The pages that follow are going to show you a better way: the autopilot way.

> *This is your captain speaking. We are currently experiencing some turbulence. Our flight has been interrupted by some present practices and routines that aren't very efficient or productive. Now that we've realized where this turbulence is coming from, we are ready to address it. We should be flying through clear skies in just a few moments, arriving safely at productivity.*

THE PATH FORWARD AND THE PREFLIGHT CHECKLIST

Hello, this is your captain speaking again. We are presently flying at twenty thousand feet on our flight from almost done to just about finished. I've turned off the fasten seatbelt sign, and you are free to move about the cabin. We are expecting a smooth flight and anticipate an on-time arrival to the beautiful city of Productivity. I hope you enjoy your flight here on Autopilot airlines.

The autopilot approach will make your position as a school leader easier. It should allow you to streamline your workflow, minimize stress, and reclaim your valuable time. Autopilot is going to help you become a more focused and organized leader by using several productivity systems and tools. How will it do this? The following chapters will examine specific strategies and systems to help move you forward:

- Email Solutions and Communication Overload (Chapter 5): We will focus on inbox strategies to help lessen the impact of

the constant drip of emails and learn how to batch and organize the information that we consistently share with families.
- Mastering Your Time and Energy (Chapter 6): We will concentrate on time saving techniques, scheduling strategies, and theme days to block our days efficiently.
- Conquering Procrastination and Perfectionism (Chapter 7): We will target methods for managing procrastination and minimizing our perfectionist tendencies. We will discover ways to remain focused even with distractions all around us.
- Automation, Delegation, and Empowerment (Chapter 8): We will hone in on automation strategies to delegate to and empower our colleagues in order to take some of the work off our plates.
- Streamlining Your Workflows (Chapter 9): We will spotlight strategies to eliminate the unnecessary, decide what's truly urgent, and organize our most critical work. We will learn how to use an old-fashioned notebook to organize everything.
- Create a Focused, Productive Environment (Chapter 10): We will pay attention to techniques for creating a culture of productivity, celebrating our wins, and creating a cave-like focused environment.
- Routines and Rituals for Success (Chapter 11): We will observe a variety of routines and rituals in action that help us with shutting down every day, overcoming that Sunday night feeling, and utilizing the full power of the summer.

The Autopilot Preflight Checklist

In order to think clearly about productivity and how we should approach our jobs, we can look at the Autopilot Preflight Checklist. This checklist can help us consider a task that we are trying to add to our already full plates, and decide whether we will tackle it. The checklist features four key questions we should ask ourselves when considering any new task or project. These are basic questions that will help us ensure that we are doing valuable tasks that make an impact.

What? We start by identifying our goal for the task and determining what we want to accomplish.

Why? This is the most important part of the checklist, as we want to determine if a goal provides any value to our day. I like to break down my goals into three categories: low, medium, and high value. I would love to fill my day with super meaningful, high-value activities, but we all know that there are days when we just need to complete some of those low-value, necessary tasks. As you are determining what to put on your to-do list, always go back to the *why* of it. Is this item helping you be purposeful?

How? Now that you've identified a goal and understand why that goal is important, you will come up with a plan to accomplish the goal. This might involve technical planning, such as determining what type of technology or resource you need to use or whether you'll need to delegate the work to someone who is better suited to complete the task. The *how* is all about developing a solid plan for moving forward.

When? The final checklist item is about establishing a timeline for accomplishing your goal. We've already brainstormed brilliant ideas for how we can improve our schools and, at one point or another, let those ideas slip away with those ill-fated words, "If only I had the time." This step is all about committing calendar time to our goals. Block off a specific day and time for when you will tackle your plan. Mark it on your calendar, and use that time wisely.

At the end of the strategy chapters in this book, you will find a preflight checklist for you to complete. You can determine what, if any, strategies from the chapter you want to try, and answer each of the four questions from the checklist.

And now, on to the autopilot strategies.

THE AUTOPILOT STRATEGIES

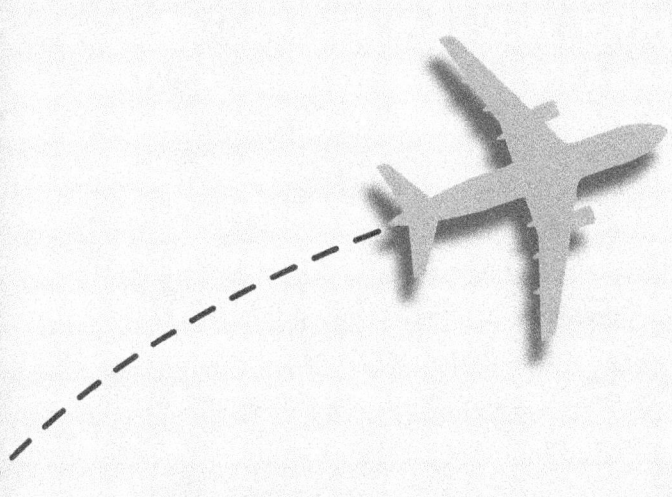

START WITH THE BASICS

EMAIL SOLUTIONS AND COMMUNICATION OVERLOAD

One of the most time-consuming tasks in a school leader's day is managing their inbox and the overwhelming flow of emails. In this chapter, you'll find strategies to help you organize your inbox, minimize time spent on emails, utilize email templates, and batch your communication.

> ### AN OPEN LETTER TO EVERYONE WHO EMAILS ME BUT DOESN'T REALLY NEED TO EMAIL ME
>
> Dear Education Vendors, Health and Safety Experts, EdTech Companies, and those Companies Trying to Sell Me Silicone Wristbands with Our School Logo on Them:
>
> I get it.

> Each of you has the ultimate solution to all of my problems. While the education profession has created its fair share of problems that need to be solved and inherited a bunch of problems from elsewhere, it has also added the problem of too many vendors trying to sell me something.
>
> My inbox is besieged each day by thirty to forty marketing emails (no exaggeration) promising the fix to all of our school problems—facilities, technology, arrival and dismissal, parent communication, and how to get our screen-printed logo on T-shirts or rubber wristbands delivered within forty-eight hours!
>
> It's all too much.
>
> I get it. You want to help by selling me something. But I don't need you to sell me anything.
>
> I'll ask you to help in a different manner.
>
> Stop emailing me. (And if you don't, I'm simply going to report your email as spam and let my email provider handle it appropriately.)
>
> Sincerely,
> Rich

To Email, or Not to Email, That Is the Question

I'm sure those that conceived the idea of email did not anticipate spam and junk mail. They probably envisioned a system designed to help us with faster and easier communication. Little did they know that their system for faster and easier communication would devolve into one of the largest time-sucks imaginable. While email should make us more efficient, it actually adds more unwanted and unnecessary communication to our plate, which impacts our own schedule. Anyone can email you at any time (given they know your email address, and I'm guessing it's on your school/district website). Your inbox is often filled with messages that you don't want or need, but you're still forced to do something about them. When email first became commonplace, it may have been seen as a novel way to communicate. Now it has become the bane of our existence. So, why don't we just eliminate it as a communication tool? The simple reason is that it actually works efficiently for certain tasks when we eliminate all of the negatives surrounding it.

Inbox Zero

I've seen the over-the-top proponents of inbox zero. A term that was initially devised as an efficiency strategy evolved into a time-consuming obsession to keep one's inbox empty at all times. I've seen the social media posts featuring snapshots of the poster's empty inbox; when I achieved it once, I was so excited that I also shared a picture of my inbox zero win. It's a great feeling.

But it's a shortsighted goal. Our inboxes fill up at an alarming rate. If I empty mine today, there will be thirty new messages awaiting me tomorrow. It seems like an uncontrollable problem. It seems like an insurmountable mess. And it is. But there are ways to better manage your inbox and approach your email overall.

Email Templates and Premail

So how much time do you spend on email on a daily basis? If you're lucky, your answer was probably somewhere around thirty to sixty minutes. This seems like a reasonable amount of time to spend on email. But if you don't have some sort of plan to attack your inbox, then your inbox just might be attacking you instead. If you answered the question honestly, you're likely spending upward of three to four hours a day on email. If you're in the worst-case scenario, your inbox is open all day, constantly calling you away from your most important work.

As a school leader, my guess is that most of the emails you receive need to be responded to. Whether it's a teacher asking a question, a parent questioning you, or someone from the central office trying to get an update, the majority of your emails will require a thoughtful response. Some emails, however, can be answered with the same response. Let's look at an example.

As an elementary school principal, I often get a deluge of emails each spring from parents with a variety of requests related to class placement for the following year. Can you place my child with their best friend? Can you make sure that my child is placed in Mrs. Perfect's classroom for next year? Or the inverse question, can you make sure that my child doesn't end up in Mr. Notsoperfect's classroom?

While in the past I would respond to each email with a carefully thought-out response, I learned through the years that a better approach was to develop an email template. It's much easier to send a blanket email with an appropriate response. Over the years, I've tailored the email template to meet the varied placement requests that may come in.

Here is my standard response:

> Thank you for your email! While we don't honor specific teacher requests or requests for certain students to be placed with your child, we do try to use all information available to find the best fit for each student.
>
> The information that you shared will be helpful as we consider student placement for next year. We will definitely note the information that you shared. Please let me know if you have any other questions.
>
> Thanks,
> Rich Czyz

This email template serves as an easy way to respond to these emails when they come in each spring. In the past, I've also sent home a message to parents and guardians as a preemptive strike against this round of emails. I like to call it *premail*. It's similar to the above message and lets parents know that we don't consider specific requests. I've learned, though, that even if I send out a preemptive message, I'm still likely to receive requests from parents, so the above template is my starting point for all responses to parents regarding class placement. Sometimes, I can respond directly with the template response, and at other times I'll need to edit slightly to address a particular request or statement within the parent email. It certainly saves a lot of time to have the template ready to go when the same types of emails keep coming in.

Likewise, once class placement information is sent out to families prior to the start of the school year, I send out a premail to head off the number of email responses requesting that I change their child's placement. It reads:

> Good morning!
>
> I wanted to remind all families that class placement and transportation information is available in the online parent portal today.
>
> Considerable time, energy, and critical thought went into determining class lists, and we have carefully considered the needs of each student as they were assigned a teacher for the school year. With this in mind, we will not consider any requests for changes to class lists at this time. Last-minute changes to one student placement can have a domino effect and begin to impact other students, student schedules, and teacher schedules, as well as disrupt the carefully thought-out placements. Thank you for your understanding.
>
> Rich Czyz

Think about the emails that you receive. Are there specific types of emails that require similar responses each time? Anything similar to what I've described above? You could also create email templates for dealing with interview requests or hiring initiatives, using something along the lines of the following:

> Thank you very much for sharing your résumé. At this time, we do not have any open positions, but we will keep your résumé on file in the event that a position does open up. Best of luck in your job search!

I use a standard email template or premails to help me save time in the following areas:

- student placement/schedules
- teacher hiring and interviews
- curriculum and instruction
- standardized assessments
- student behavior and discipline

Consider setting up some email templates to help you avoid thinking about email responses. Consider establishing some premail templates that you can send out to avoid receiving emails in the first place. The fewer emails landing in your inbox, the more time you have to dedicate to more important pursuits.

> **CONTROL PANEL CHECK: SCHEDULE EMAILS**
>
> Most email providers have a great function that allows you to schedule your emails. This function is a lifesaver for me. While I try to maintain the sanctity of my nonwork hours by not bringing work home, there are times when I need to prepare a message for someone after hours. Maybe I didn't quite get to it during the day or I just thought of it. Even though I might write the message after hours, I also want to honor the

> sanctity of others' home lives. That means I'll always schedule it for the next morning at eight.
>
> I'm bound by this rule. No emails sent after 4:30 p.m. Everything scheduled for the following day at eight.
>
> Scheduling emails can also help as you batch your work. I write the Friday Focus, my weekly newsletter/calendar to staff, in monthly batches and schedule them to send each week. Same for parent updates. The other bonus to scheduling emails is that sometimes you forget to add something or the information changes—and when the email hasn't been sent yet, it can be edited.
>
> Don't frantically send emails. Take your time. Do them right. Schedule them.

Avoid Email Tag

You are getting ready to plan your monthly professional development session for staff, and you want to connect with one of the district instructional coaches to find out what type of strategy you should plan. You send an initial email, and then start a series of emails that looks something like this:

> You (first email): Good morning, what type of instructional strategy should we highlight for our professional development session next month?
>
> Instructional Coach (second email): I was thinking that we might be able to highlight something from the new math curriculum or follow-up on the ELA writing strategy we shared back in October. Which one do you think we should do?

You (third email): I've talked to staff and I think they have a good handle on the writing strategy that was shared. I definitely think we should focus on the new math curriculum. Do you think we should share a strategy for word problems or focus more on number sense?

Instructional Coach (fourth email): Either of those would be good, but I think that teachers also need some help with how to access the online resources with the new curriculum. What do you think?

You are knee-deep in a game of email tag. You've already taken about ten minutes to send and receive multiple emails, and there is no end in sight. This game of email tag will take time, attention, and focus away from other important tasks. The series of emails could stretch over hours or days. There has to be a better way. Email was heralded as the technology tool that we all needed, something that was going to make our lives easier. We all jumped on board and tackled every piece of communication with email. However, email is not the answer to all of our communication needs.

There are several solutions to the email tag problem and one solution, as old school as they come, is sitting down with the person one-on-one, or picking up the phone and calling them. Imagine how much easier the above email conversation could have been if it were a real-life conversation. Instead of communicating back and forth over email spanning several hours, you sit down with the person for fifteen minutes and hash out the details of the next PD session. A phone call also works perfectly in this situation. You talk with the person, ask all of the questions you need to, and agree upon all of the relevant details before you hang up the phone. It takes ten minutes: no mess, no fuss.

Email can be a tremendous tool when you are trying to accomplish certain things, but it can also hinder our ability to be successful or productive. Let's think about another example. Most of you have been in this position before. You need to schedule a meeting of the school climate committee, so you send an email to the five members:

> Good morning everyone,
>
> We need to schedule our next meeting of the school climate committee. Does next Tuesday at 8:00 a.m. work for everyone?
>
> Thanks,
> Rich

Just like a math word problem on probability, we might ask how many possible emails could be sent to respond to this initial message.

> Team Member #1: Tuesday at 8:00 a.m. is perfect! See you then!
>
> Team Member #2: I can't be there until 8:15 a.m. Does that work?
>
> Team Member #3: I'm on a personal day on Tuesday. Can we meet on Thursday?

Before you know it, the messages come in like clockwork. You've got a thirty-seven-message email chain that only determines that getting these five members of the team together is as challenging as the original NASA engineers trying to organize space flight. It doesn't have to be this way. After all, scheduling is not rocket science.

Scheduling in this way does nothing but take up your precious time and the time of everyone else on the team. There are several scheduling apps that can help. Something like Calendly helps all members of the team share their availability in an easy-to-use interface. As the team leader, you can then pick the date and time that works best according to everyone's calendar. I also find that it is helpful to share my work calendar with all of those that may need access to it. If I'm trying to meet with a single person, I may just share my calendar with them and ask them to pick a date/time that coordinates with their schedule as well.

For example, when I am scheduling end-of-year summative review meetings for more than forty staff members, I set up appointment slots and share my Google Calendar, asking each staff member to pick the time that works best for them. Ninety percent of these meetings go off without a hitch. This method saves hundreds of emails from going back and forth between me and my colleagues trying to organize a schedule. It simply makes sense to work smarter and not harder in this regard.

Email tag can be a time-suck that drains you of the energy needed to focus on what matters. Leave the scheduling to automated scheduling assistants or an app like Calendly or Google Calendar. Sometimes, your work conversations are best saved for human interaction and not emails. Avoid unnecessary email chains by having an actual conversation with someone to solve your problems, strategize, or collaborate. It will be more fun interacting with a human being anyway, rather than your computer or phone.

Get a Bigger BOAT!

Now we've shared a couple of methods for minimizing the number of emails that you are sending and receiving, but I'm sure that your inbox is still filled to capacity. It might seem that you actually need a bigger inbox to handle all of the email that is sent your way each day. That's the problem with email. It's just never-ending. It's not as if you'll catch up one day, and suddenly everyone will stop emailing you.

While you don't need a bigger inbox, what you do need is a bigger BOAT.

One of my favorite movies of all time is *Jaws*. My love affair with the movie began when I was a kid, and to this day I'm still scared at all the right times. It's a masterpiece of cinema.

Brody utters one of the movie's great lines after he sees the humongous shark up close for the first time. He backs into the boat's cabin and calmly says to Quint, "You're gonna need a bigger boat."

When we think of our inbox as *Jaws*, we realize that we do need a bigger BOAT: Blocked Off Answering Time. Our BOATs are a series of times blocked off throughout the day to answer our emails. While we can keep our inbox open all day and respond every time someone wants to take up our valuable time by sending an email, this method completely defeats the purpose of staying organized and productive. Instead, block off several times during your day, and only answer emails during these times.

I like to tackle my inbox first thing in the morning, but at that time I'm often struggling to ensure that I have subs for every class. Instead, I usually give myself about thirty minutes to answer emails right after morning arrival. I try to stick to checking and responding to emails about three times a day.

My BOAT schedule looks like this:

> 8:00–8:30 a.m. or 9:00–9:30 a.m.—About thirty minutes of checking and responding to emails that have been sent overnight

> 12:00–12:30 p.m—Another 15–20 minutes of checking and responding to emails and catching up on any morning correspondence

> 3:40–4:10 p.m.—Another 15–20 minutes of checking and responding to anything before I leave for the day

Any emails for staff composed during the third BOAT are scheduled to go out the following morning at eight. All email is checked and composed by 4:30 p.m., and I do not check it again until the following morning. I want to respect everyone's boundaries, including my own, my family's, and my colleagues'. No emails after 4:30 p.m.! On a good day, I'll only spend about an hour checking and responding to my school inbox. The BOATs allow me to focus on other tasks, rather than be trapped by email all day. When we leave email open all day and respond immediately to each and every response, we are sending the message that we are constantly available at the whim of whoever wants to send us something.

Keep in mind that it is OK to let people know when you will be responding to emails as well. You can include a tagline at the bottom of your email that states:

> I usually check email three times a day. Please expect a response during one of these times (8:00–8:30 a.m., 12:00–12:30 p.m., or 3:40–4:10 p.m.). I will respond to your email within twenty-four hours. Thank you for your understanding.

It is also helpful to notify people when you will not be responding to emails. I always utilize the autoresponder function of my email when I am on a personal day and won't be responding to any emails. A simple response can go a long way to notifying staff, parents, and others that you won't be responding to emails for a certain period of time:

> Thank you for your email. I am currently out of the office and will not begin responding to emails until Monday.
>
> Thanks,
> Rich Czyz

If you are going for productivity and efficiency, it's never a good idea to be at the mercy of your inbox. When you are opening your inbox, you are usually trying to check off items on someone else's to-do list. Minimize the time that you check and respond to emails. Don't battle with your inbox. Get a bigger BOAT, and leave your valuable time for something else.

Organize Your Inbox

We have covered a lot of ground with regards to email and your inbox. I will share one more strategy that has helped me to tame email. One of the biggest issues I used to run into was rereading emails a half dozen times before I decided to do anything with them. These could be difficult emails that required a thoughtful response, emails that included a question I didn't know the answer to, or requests that needed to be delegated to someone else.

Have you ever struggled with this problem? If so, I have developed a simple way to organize my inbox that helps to address the challenge. My inbox home screen is split into four sections. On the full left side of my screen is my inbox. This is where all of my new emails come in. On the right side of my inbox, I have three sections: Today, This Week, and Reference.

Any email that I receive that does not require a response will go into an appropriate folder (Curriculum, Interviews/Hiring, Facilities, Technology, etc.). Any email that requires a simple answer, I will try to answer it immediately, then file it in the appropriate folder. If I read an email that does not warrant an immediate response, I will move the email to either the Today or This Week sections. If an email is in either section, I know that I need to respond within that given time frame. I might have three to four emails within each section at any given time. Once I do send a response, I move the email to the appropriate folder.

The reference folder is used to hold emails that I need to reference often. For example, each year our HR department sends out a link to our district observation chart. This chart shows all of the teacher observations that I am responsible for and gets updated several times throughout the year. I keep the initial email in my reference section so that I can refer back to it whenever a round of observations has passed. It makes it easier than going back to search within my inbox or folders to find the original email. It's always right there. The same goes for the district security drill chart, which needs to be updated each month after we hold our monthly fire drill and security drill. The reference section serves as the perfect holding tank for any messages or links that need to be accessed on a regular basis.

A cautionary note about this system: It works for me. However, I know that it may not work for you. I've seen those people who constantly have 23,798 emails in their inbox and can still easily find something using the email search function. It doesn't work for me. I tried to find a system that helps me to minimize the number of times that I read an email. I want to read it once and address it. While I'm suggesting very specific ideas that you can use to automate and be more productive, I believe that it's also important to experiment, explore, and find a method that works for you.

Until I went into the settings on my work email, I had no idea that you could even separate your inbox into up to five different sections. Most email providers provide a plethora of options that are designed to make you more productive. You just have to play around with the features to see what works for you and what doesn't. Don't be afraid to click. Try something. If it doesn't work, you can always go back to the default settings for your email.

> **CONTROL PANEL CHECK: FAQS**
>
> How many times do you find yourself answering the same questions over and over again? You had a conversation last week with a new parent about how the lunch program works. Now you are talking to another parent (whose child has been in the building for six years) who still doesn't know how to add lunch money to their child's account.
>
> Anytime you are answering the same questions over and over again, it's time for an FAQ. It's simple to do. Open a blank document, and start typing out all of those repeat questions that you or the main office staff are constantly answering.

> Type out some detailed and thoughtful responses. Keep all of the frequently asked questions and answers in one digital document that parents can find easily on your school website. Add more questions and answers as they come up. Keep the FAQ as a living and breathing document easily accessible to families.
>
> Get those FAQs out there and save yourself some time and some breath.

Find Me a Find, Batch Me a Batch

Strong communication is one of the most important attributes that a school leader can possess. It's important to communicate with all stakeholders: students, staff, and families. How you communicate may vary by person. What I may be comfortable with might be very different from another school leader. Some may prefer to send email communication such as newsletters or weekly/monthly updates. Some school leaders may utilize their phone-blast system, sending daily or weekly all-calls to students and families. Some school leaders may lead the way with the latest social media app, communicating with parents and students on their own turf. You may find that each family has their own preferences when it comes to communication.

No matter which communication tool you utilize, the one automation strategy that you'll want to utilize is batching and scheduling your communication. I stick with the tried and true Smore newsletter to share information with staff and families. I've been utilizing Smore for more than ten years, and it's an easy way for me to quickly engage staff and families while gathering data on the back end to know exactly how many people my messages are reaching. The most important part of my communication strategy is batching. It's quite a time-saver and allows me to save time and energy when I'm preparing communications.

Each week, I send staff a Friday Focus via Smore with a funny meme, calendar updates, and several instructional strategies that I've found online. I like to batch these, creating several at once to save time. Smore makes it easy to copy and paste one newsletter to another, so once I create a list of calendar events on a newsletter, I just start eliminating events for each week as it passes.

For example, our end-of-year calendar gets extremely busy. For the Friday Focus I sent out on the last day of May, I created a list of June events:

Mon, June 3
- Elem honors band concert dress rehearsal
- Elem honors band concert (evening)
- First-grade picnic (12–3 p.m.)

Tues, June 4
- SCHOOL CLOSED for students (PD day for staff)

Wed, June 5
- Aware Because We Care day

Thurs, June 6
- Field Day (rain date)
- Second-grade picnic (12–3 p.m.)
- PD LIFT 4 p.m.

Fri, June 7
- Fourth-grade picnic (12–3 p.m.)

Mon, June 10
- Third-grade picnic (12–3 p.m.)

Tues, June 11
- Fifth-grade jobs picnic (12–3 p.m.)

Wed, June 12
- Kindergarten end-of-year awards/celebration 9:30 a.m.–12:30 p.m.

Thurs, June 13
- Staff meeting 3:45 p.m.

Fri, June 14
- Fifth-grade middle-school visit

Tues, June 18
- Fifth-grade moving-up ceremony and party

Wed, June 19
- SCHOOL CLOSED

Thurs, June 20
- Last day
- Student awards assemblies
- Fifth-grade vs. staff kickball game
- Fifth-grade clap-out

I then copied and pasted the newsletter, and simply eliminated any dates that had already passed. I kept doing this throughout the month.

Does it take some time up front to create the initial calendar? Absolutely. But do I save a ton of time on the back end by having the whole calendar in place? You betcha. Batching the newsletters allows me to create several weeks of information while spending a minimal amount of time within my schedule. While it takes about fifteen to twenty minutes to create one newsletter at a time, I might be able to crank out five to six newsletters in just over an hour. I don't need to produce another newsletter for several weeks. It's time well spent.

I do the same for parent communications. I include a YES (Yardville Elementary School) This Week newsletter for parents, in which I also share important calendar dates (created from the same list I use for teachers minus the teacher-only events), relevant parent info, and pictures of what's happening in the school. Parents stay connected. When I'm in Smore newsletter mode, I might produce more than ten Friday Focus and YES This Week editions over a ninety-minute span. While ninety minutes seems like a lot of investment for a single day, the benefit is long-term: no more newsletters for several weeks.

I also batch the dissemination of such newsletters. I use several tools to communicate with parents, including our district messaging system (School Messenger), which delivers the newsletters via email and text message. I also use a messaging app (Talking Points), which translates the message into home languages for families who speak a different language at home. I'll schedule each week's message and link to the newsletter several weeks ahead of time. Batching is all about making an up-front commitment to save time down the road. You'll be able to utilize the time worry-free later on.

The added benefit of using Smore is that the newsletter is live. If a date changes or you want to add more information to a particular week's newsletter, you simply go in and update the specific week. The link for that week remains the same, so there's no need to go back and change the scheduled email sharing of the link.

> **SYSTEMS CHECK**
>
> What other things do you do that are repetitive and lend themselves to batching?

Preflight Checklist for Email Solutions and Communication

- ❏ What strategy from this chapter would you like to try?
- ❏ Why? (your true north)
- ❏ How? (your plan)
- ❏ When? (your timeline)

MASTERING YOUR TIME AND ENERGY

Entrepreneur and performance coach Michael Altshuler said, "The bad news is time flies. The good news is you're the pilot." Our time is one of the most precious commodities we have as administrators. We need to protect it. In this part of the book, you'll find strategies to tackle the tough tasks, organize your office hours, build gap time into your day so you are not derailed by emergencies, and design theme days to streamline your work.

Eat a Frog (or a Bigger Frog)

As a school leader, you have been face-to-face with an uncomfortable situation at some point in your educational career. Maybe it was a conversation that you had to have with a colleague. Maybe it was a meeting with a parent where you had to tell them something that they didn't want to hear. Maybe it was a task that you just absolutely hate doing.

I was once at a training program with other principals, and one talked about eating the frog, getting it over with, and moving on with your day. I had no idea what he was talking about until I looked it up. I discovered that Mark Twain once said, "If it's your job to eat a frog, it's best to do it first thing in the morning. And if it's your job to eat two frogs, it's best to eat the biggest one first."

My frogs usually involve difficult conversations with parents, whether in person or via a phone call. I always feel like these conversations are hanging over my head. I dread them. I can't sleep the night before. It's the worst possible feeling. Still, I try to schedule the meeting first thing in the morning, because I have found that sometimes the meeting goes better than anticipated. I have come to fear the worst, and it's rarely as bad as I thought it would be. Sometimes, it's much worse than expected, but then it's over, and I can get on with the rest of my day.

So, if you have to eat a frog, eat it first thing. Get it out of the way and leave the rest of the day for your most productive self. And if you have to eat two frogs, be sure to tackle the largest one first.

The Two-Minute Rule

When we are besieged by any number of tasks, it's important to accomplish them quickly. I live by the two-minute rule. If a task is going to take less than two minutes, I do it right away. No need to put it on the back burner for later in the day. This might be an important rule for email or other simple tasks. Don't waste time by thinking about how to accomplish some of those easy goals. Just get them out of the way immediately. Two-minute rule, over and done with.

The Touch-It-Once Rule

Paperwork can be an overwhelming part of a school administrator's job. There are many paper tasks that can eat up your time. Think about all of the paperwork that fills your day:

- work orders
- purchase orders

- weekly payroll
- daily attendance lists
- discipline slips

The list goes on and on. With any physical paperwork that comes across your desk, I want you to implement a simple rule. It's the touch-it-once rule. Whenever that paperwork is in your hands for the first time, address it. Don't just look at it and then put it back on your table for later. Handle it right then and there. Touch it once.

I'll give the prime example from my day that often trips me up. Anytime a purchase order needs to be approved, I need to sign it and also go into the online payment system to digitally approve it. I can't tell you the number of times that I've signed the paper and forgotten to go into the online system for digital approval. Many times, I'll put the paper down after it's handed to me and wait until later to get it done. Later never comes. I'll have my assistant remind me several hours later, "Did you approve that purchase order?"

The best method is to touch it once. Get it done as soon as you can. Don't waste time on the administrative minutiae. Sign it. Seal it. Deliver it. Touch it once.

> **CONTROL PANEL CHECK: SELF-EMAILS**
>
> A few moments of quiet reflection can lead to a motivational morning. It's really a simple action that can help you start off your day on the right foot. Take the last five to ten minutes of your day to reflect on your day. Review what you have accomplished. Take a look at your to-do list for the day, and decide what you want to move forward for tomorrow. Then type a "good morning" email to yourself. It's an email that you will schedule to be delivered to your own inbox the next morning. It can be part inspirational, part motivational, and part to-do. (Think, "Hey Rich! Great job yesterday. Let's get right to work

> this morning on Chapter 2. Don't forget that wonderful idea you had about bento box productivity.")

Bento Box Productivity

Organizing a to-do list can be tough. You add all of the tasks to your list, regardless of their value proposition or importance to you. Think about two tasks that might appear on your to-do list:

- email reminder to staff with the PD schedule for next Friday
- email parent to discuss discipline issue with student

This seems like one of those scenario-based questions that they give you when you interview for an administrative position. Which task should you do first? While the PD schedule email will impact more people, the parent email is more timely. So which do you do first? This is part of the problem with a checklist of items. Everything has the same importance. You could prioritize your list by adding a ranking of importance, or you could re-list them in a specific order. I'm going to suggest a different strategy for organizing your to-do list that may help.

If you are familiar with a bento box, you know that it's a container for a meal that holds several different separated sections with different types of food. The term *bento* comes from Chinese slang meaning *convenient*. With this idea in mind, I developed a bento box organizer for my daily goals that can help you to prioritize your tasks.

You can try using the Bento Box Productivity Sheet (find the link for all resources on the last page of the book) to organize your daily goals. The sheet starts with one large box at the top and four smaller boxes of varying sizes at the bottom of the page. This format serves as the perfect way to organize your day. Instead of listing all of your to-do list items with equal gravity, the bento box allows you to focus on three to five goals for the day and provides the space to organize them in such a way that you know exactly what takes priority. Your highest priority task goes in the largest box, and other tasks are ordered using the decreasing size of the other boxes.

Let's examine how the page might be used. Let's say you are trying to accomplish several goals today. Your list looks like this:

- send out parent letter for end of year student event
- complete class placement lists for next year
- organize next year's schedule
- email facilities director with a classroom request for next year
- classroom walk-throughs—fourth and fifth grade

This list looks pretty thorough, and these all seem like high-value tasks that you are trying to accomplish. In order to organize the bento box, you need to decide which is the most important task to focus on today. You can organize these tasks in order using the bento box and develop laser focus for the day. Follow the items from one through five, and don't stop until you've completed each item.

Utilizing the bento box to organize your daily goals, while simultaneously building in time on your schedule, will allow you to actually accomplish your daily goals. The bento box strategy allows you to minimize your number of daily goals so that they are manageable, while also setting you up to finish the most important of your goals.

The Power of Breaks

As an administrator, there are many days when you are going full speed all day long. You'll look up at the clock to see that it's 3:00 p.m. Dismissal is in twenty-five minutes, and you've had to pee since nine. You've been so busy, however, that you've forgotten to use the bathroom. Going at this pace is not mentally or physically healthy.

You have to build in periodic breaks for yourself throughout the day to ensure your own mental health and physical wellness. Here are some fun ways to incorporate short breaks during your day. They will help to keep you motivated and on track while you try to tackle everything on your to-do list.

Take a nature walk. Just getting outside for five minutes can provide a wonderful boost to your day. When I am heading to another part of our school, I often walk outside the long way around the school to go back inside and into a classroom on the other side of the building. This provides a couple of minutes and a peaceful moment before jumping back into my task list.

Try some desk yoga. Incorporate some light stretches at your desk in between daily activities. You don't need to roll out the yoga mat, or go full downward dog, but even some light stretches can reinvigorate your day.

Act like a kid and color. Get one of those awesome adult coloring books and a box of colored pencils. Spend just a few minutes each day with some mindful coloring and by the end of the week, you'll have an awesome masterpiece. You'll find the activity to be quite relaxing and refreshing, especially after a really difficult task.

Phone a friend. Whenever you're feeling a little overwhelmed or stressed, call up a colleague or friend to share a quick moment or laugh at a recent situation you found yourself in. I always had my go-to phone call whenever I needed a break. There were two other principals in my district who I would call if I needed a moment of distraction. When at your wit's end, phone a friend.

Visit the "fun" classrooms. I'm assuming that all of your classrooms are fun, but if you are like me, you find some classrooms to be more fun than others. Whenever I need a break, I'll often go visit our preschool classrooms because those students are always so excited to see me. It provides an instant boost to my day, especially when it's been a rough one. Art is another class I love to visit. It's always inspiring to see what students are creating.

Mindful splashing and washing. When things are escalating during your day, take a minute and hit the bathroom. Mindfully splash some cold water over your face, and take a moment to slowly wash your hands. Let the moment literally wash over you. Enjoy it for what it is, and know that you at least just killed some germs.

> **CONTROL PANEL CHECK: CALENDAR REMINDERS TO GET OUT AND ABOUT**
>
> There are times when you will get stuck at your desk or your computer. It can be an urgent email message that just came in from your supervisor, or a parent phone call that went thirty minutes longer than you expected. Maybe you are trying to handle a discipline issue and have to talk to multiple students to figure it all out.
>
> Whatever the reason is, it's keeping you from doing the work you were meant to be doing: getting out and about in classrooms visiting with students and teachers. Have you ever found yourself trapped in your office? Don't get stuck any longer.
>
> Set up calendar reminders several times a day to ensure that you are able to get out and see what's taking place in the school. Not only does this provide a walking break away from your desk, but you can check out the meaningful instruction and learning taking place in your school.
>
> Set those reminders. Get up and out of the office many times a day.

Leave Space in the Margin

If you were to look at my digital calendar, there are days that you would see it completely filled from beginning to end. These days are always quite adventurous, and they usually go quickly. Anytime any kind of fire arises during the day, whether it be an unexpected fire alarm, a student discipline problem, a facilities snafu, or even another item from the schedule, something else now needs to be minimized or forgotten completely.

We know that, on any given day, emergencies will arise. And that is exactly why we should plan for emergencies. I like to leave white space within my schedule to accommodate the things that pop up unexpectedly. There are several different strategies you can utilize to plan for white space in your schedule.

One-for-one white space. For every meeting or activity that you build into your schedule, block off an equal amount of time in your schedule too. For example, if you schedule a parent meeting for thirty minutes on Tuesday morning, make sure you also put a thirty-minute white space block on your schedule for Tuesday. This strategy will allow you to utilize about half of your schedule and dedicate half of it to open time blocks. It won't always be possible to accommodate your schedule this way, but it certainly helps when you are inundated with emergencies.

Buffer space. Attach a buffer space to the end of each scheduled meeting or activity. Are you scheduled to attend a virtual district curriculum meeting for an hour this afternoon? Make sure to attach a fifteen- or twenty-minute time slot at the end in case the meeting goes long or in case you need to clarify some of the information with a colleague. If the meeting ends up going ten minutes short, you now have an extra thirty-minute window to accomplish something on your to-do list that you weren't expecting to get to that day.

Daily disaster downtime. You know that disasters are going to happen. It doesn't matter how well you plan, how organized or proactive you are, or how you schedule your day; the disasters will find you. Build in an hour-long disaster downtime each day. The hour downtime with nothing else scheduled gives you extra time for when those catastrophes hit. Give each time block a cool disaster nickname on your calendar. Some of my favorites are Meltdown Monday, Tornado Tuesday, Wildfire Wednesday (or Hurricane Humpday), Turbulent

Thursday, and Fiasco Friday. Not only will you have extra time to handle all that comes your way, but anyone looking at your calendar will ask fun questions like, "What's Fiasco Friday? Can you tell me more about that?"

Schedule a status meeting (with yourself). Status meetings are designed to provide an update on any current projects you and others may be working on. By scheduling a status meeting with yourself, you can review your progress in any number of areas. Use the time to review important student-learning data, update progress on teacher observations, evaluate walk-through data, or check résumés for potential teaching candidates. Remember, the point of opening up time in your schedule is to ensure that you are getting to meaningful work and not just fighting fires all day. You can schedule self-status meetings once on Monday morning, once again on Wednesday afternoon, and a third one on Friday.

Open office hours. Meeting with and having conversations with staff is just one of the things that gets lost in the shuffle when you have emergencies popping up all day. Have you ever been in a meeting with a staff member in your office when suddenly you are interrupted by another staff member with some kind of disaster? I feel like it happens all the time. Now, you could have a hard-and-fast rule that if someone is in your office you can't be interrupted, but we all know that's not always feasible when you're responsible for hundreds or thousands of students. As the lone administrator in my building, sometimes I have to get up to excuse myself. Build in an open office hour several times a week to give teachers the ability to pop in or schedule a time with you. You can use the time to answer staff questions, check in after a walk-through, or collaborate on an idea. Again, white space can help in any number of ways.

While it may seem counterproductive to efficiency, scheduling open times within your schedule can actually help to aid your productivity. Worst-case scenario, you have time to deal with the unexpected.

Best-case scenario, you have open times to accomplish work that you haven't gotten to. It's a huge win-win scenario for you.

Take Advantage of Early and Late Hours

It's easier to accomplish tasks when you won't be interrupted. You need to be able to find times during the day when you can achieve a feeling of quiet focus. This is where early and late hours come in.

My normal starting time is 8:00 a.m. Teachers need to start their day by 8:25 a.m. Some early goers are there as early as I am. Therefore, in order to have some quiet, focused time to accomplish something specific, I may arrive at school as early as 7:00 a.m. The only other person in the building at that time is our custodian, who is also trying to get through his checklist unbothered. I know that if I sit and focus from seven to eight in the morning, I can truly get a lot done. There are no phone calls, no other adults to come in and interrupt. As long as I can focus, I will have an untouched window of time to do what I need to do.

I utilize Friday afternoons in the same manner. Everyone is usually gone just a few minutes after students as the weekend approaches. I find that this is the perfect time to get caught up or plan for the coming week without being interrupted. While you may spend a few more minutes on a Friday afternoon before heading home, it's time that you'll save not worrying over the weekend, or needing to frantically prep for early Monday morning.

Anytime that you can have some peace and quiet during those early or late hours is going to be beneficial to getting things done.

Use Your Time Wisely—Schedule Office Hours

You may abide by an open-door policy. If your door is open all day for anyone to bring any problem to you, they most certainly will. The trick to keeping your you-time to yourself, though, is to better manage your office hours and your availability.

You can't always be available. It's simply not possible with the amount of work that you need to do. But you do still want to be available to your colleagues to collaborate, problem solve, and connect. One of the best ways to do this is to think critically about how you deploy your office hours. I'll share several strategies below, and you can figure out which works best for you.

Open office hours. Set aside a number of hours each week that you are available to meet with colleagues. Maybe you send out a calendar invite for open office hours every day at 10:30 a.m. Colleagues can come join you on a first-come-first-serve basis to discuss students, curriculum, or any other topic they might need to chat about. The beauty of the open office hour format is that people are not interrupting your more important work. You've set the time and made yourself available. Now you just have to be in your office for that length of time. If no one shows up, then you have time to work on some of the minutiae. Don't work on anything too stressful, though, so that if a colleague suddenly appears at your door, you can immediately drop whatever it was you were working on.

It is key to figure out an open office hour schedule that works within the rest of your time blocks. Make sure the hours work for you. This is the perfect example of building time into your schedule to save you time in the long run. If someone comes to you outside of office hours with something that is not critical, simply ask them to join you during your office hours.

I know exactly what you are thinking right now. In my building, teachers only have a specific prep time during which they'd be free to meet with me on a given day. If I set up an office hour that doesn't coincide with their schedule, it won't work. But there's an easy fix. Establish an open office hour in the morning or afternoon before students start or once they go home for the day, or set up an open office hour that coincides with teacher lunches.

Dedicate certain times to certain problems. One of the specific time-blocking strategies that I use with my schedule is holding help sessions for topics that usually require lots of questions or meeting time. For example, each year in October, teachers must submit their student growth objectives (SGOs) so that I can review and approve them. These are designed by each teacher to track a significant data-driven goal for each student and to report back on each student's growth at the end of the year. Teachers always have a million questions about their SGOs. I set up several different SGO help sessions just prior to the due date. Teachers can attend the help sessions to ask questions, to have me double-check their numbers, or to provide feedback.

Trying to find a common time that works for all teachers can be difficult. Some teachers are early birds who arrive in time to get stuff done before school because they have after-school commitments. Other teachers are sprinting through the door right at 8:25 a.m. because they have obligations to start the day. I try to vary the times that I offer the help sessions by including both before and after-school times, as well as times that might work during the day.

Pop-up office hours. Schedules are designed in such a way that it can be difficult to find common time to meet with teachers outside of their daily prep time. If their room is on the other side of the building from your office, and they're coming to you, it could take a few minutes for them to get there. By the time they come to you, ask their question, discuss a problem/solution, or share an idea, then walk back to their classroom, they only have a few minutes of prep time left. If other teachers share the same prep time, there might not be enough time for you or them. Instead, offer pop-up meeting times. We have several standing desks in the hallways for student/staff use. Go to where the teachers are. Set up a standing desk and a standing invite for a pop-up meeting in the hallway during teacher prep times. It sends a message of commitment to staff that you are going to them. It also makes it easier for them and allows them a few more minutes to get their daily task list done. Set up regular pop-up meetings where teachers can connect.

While it may take a few more minutes out of your schedule, it will certainly be appreciated by your colleagues.

Of course, if you are meeting with teachers in the hallway, you may be concerned about privacy when discussing personal matters with the teacher. While the pop-up meetings can offer a chance to share an idea, discuss a curriculum question, or collaborate on a project, this time is probably not useful for any private conversations. If a teacher comes to a pop-up meeting to discuss something of a private nature, schedule a time to meet with them in the confines of your office.

Standing check-ins. When I started my career, I worked in a K–5 building of more than one thousand students, with more than one hundred staff members. Because the building was brand-new, the principal had the opportunity to hire half of the new staff while retaining about half of the staff from her previous building. While this was a great opportunity to create a specific culture within the building, the principal was faced with mentoring about fifteen brand-new teachers in their first-ever jobs, including me. I didn't appreciate this at the time, but now I recognize the time and effort that goes into mentoring new teachers. Novice teachers are going to have a lot of questions—and they should. I try to set up a standing meeting with new teachers on a regular basis to check in: *How's it going? What questions do you have? What do you need from me?* In addition, you can cover topics of relevance to the teachers as they come up during the year. November is parent-teacher conferences. Share some strategies with novice teachers about interacting with parents.

It may be difficult to find a time that works best for you and all novice teachers, but it's important to make sure that you can do these check-ins with a small group. The camaraderie that these new teachers will develop together is important, and teachers will have similar questions when dealing with things for the first time. If you work in a large setting (similar to my first job), set up a handful of standing meetings with three to five teachers at a time. If you only have one new teacher that you are working with, try to pair them with a second- or third-year teacher who you think might benefit from the meetings.

I can also suggest a few other options that might provide some flexibility around meetings and communication:

- *Virtual meetings.* Set up recurring virtual times where teachers can log on to a virtual meeting app (Google Meet, Zoom, etc.) and touch base with you. Virtual meetings provide flexibility for everyone.
- *Team messaging.* Set up a team messaging app (like Slack) for your staff where people can share information, send messages, and ask questions. Allowing everyone to see responses to questions may eliminate the need for some meetings.
- *Email meeting of the day.* I find that sometimes everyone has similar questions on a timely topic. I might send an email out to all staff with a reminder or clarification if I get a number of similar questions. It just makes it easier on everyone and sends out a clear, consistent message.
- *Walking meetings.* Set up a biweekly or monthly walk-and-talk where you and colleagues can walk and review/reflect on certain topics. It lets you get your steps in for the day, and serves as a great forum for conversation.

My Dream Schedule

I once had a request from our central office team to schedule a meeting during one of our busiest times of the school year. The way the request was worded made it seem like each building administrator had nothing but free time built into our day. After I briefly complained about the poorly worded communication, I joked with our front-office staff about what my imagined schedule (with nothing but free time) might look like. Here is what I came up with:

8:00–8:30	Daily staffing puzzle
8:30–9:10	Arrival puzzle
9:10–10:00	Mr. Czyz's royal breakfast
10:00–10:30	Morning yoga routine
10:30–11:00	Morning appeal that all goes well for the remainder of the day
11:00–12:00	Lunch hour (yeah right!)
12:00–12:45	Daily thinking time
12:45–1:30	Afternoon nap
1:30–2:00	Afternoon stretching/calisthenics
2:00–2:45	Other administrator tasks as assigned
2:45–3:15	Prepare for dismissal
3:15–4:00	Afternoon appeal to hope buses arrive on time/dismissal

Any of you who run a building know that none of this stuff actually happens. The only full lunch hour I've ever had has come calmly in the confines of summer. Some aspects of the above schedule do happen, like the daily staffing puzzle each morning or my hoping and praying that buses arrive on time in the afternoon.

While this seems like a completely outlandish schedule for a school administrator, there might actually be something to this. While our complete schedule may not look like this parody, we could implement certain aspects of it to help keep us sane. Remember the idea behind this book is to streamline our work, while also taking away the stress and anxiety that comes from our overwhelming job duties. We can incorporate some of these activities on a regular basis to help improve our mental state.

I'll lead off with several what-if questions. What if we incorporated some daily thinking time into our schedules? What if we built in time for afternoon stretching or yoga? We can actually do some of these things with students and staff to help strike more of a wellness balance for ourselves and those we are in charge of. If we are eliminating some of the busywork, and making more time for more important pursuits, why not consider some of these dream schedule items?

Since I love writing, I started the Secret Society of Writers a few years ago. It was a club for our most passionate third-, fourth-, and fifth-grade writers. We held secret meetings, talked in code, and met once or twice a month to write together and share our writing with each other. Some students produced novels. Some created comic books or graphic novels. Some made picture books. It was a really meaningful use of my time, and something that I really enjoyed. The only reason I was able to do it was because I was able to make time for it. What would you build into your dream schedule? Think clearly about how you can make time for some of those activities.

Theme Days

Constantly context shifting during our day takes away focus, and keeps us from doing our best work. We often are forced to shift tasks through no fault of our own. Planning to keep to one track during the day can help us to be more organized and focused in a way that lets us get all similar tasks done in one fell swoop.

Having a theme day can help you set a focus for your day and group similar tasks together. Try utilizing these theme days to organize focused work:

Mentor Monday. It's important to provide mentorship to new teachers. It's also one of the priorities that can completely fall off the table when there are a million other things going on. Set up Mentor Monday meetings with new teachers every week to check in, share some insight, and provide resources. New teachers will appreciate the scheduled time and routine of a weekly meeting. It doesn't have to last long; even ten minutes can be a perfect amount of time to check in and make sure that the novice teacher has everything they need to move forward in their role. Establishing a day to do this makes sure that mentorship does not fall off of the table. Mentor Monday makes mentorship a priority.

Tech-Free Tuesday. Plan a no-office day, and minimize your own technology use for the day while also promoting limited tech use for staff and students. Encourage analog activities like reading, writing, drawing, hands-on science activities, math games, and board games. Avoid screen fatigue. While you'll need to check email once or twice during the day, also try to keep to analog administrative tasks. Complete all those to-do list items that don't require technology. Get out and about. Model tech-free usage within the building and create a culture of creativity.

Tech Tuesday. Alternate Tech-Free Tuesday with Tech Tuesday and promote a new tech tool with staff in a brief session before school. Then visit classrooms and help teachers incorporate the tech tool into their lessons. Encourage teachers and students to explore new technology programs or software or implement new tech strategies throughout the day. Share a document at the end of the day that features pictures of Tech Tuesday happenings, and share links to some of the new tech tools that teachers are using.

Walk-Through Wednesday. Schedule your classroom visitations and walk-throughs for a single day. Build the routine of conducting walk-throughs each week. Schedule your classroom visits in the morning, and schedule follow-up time to share feedback with teachers. Creating the ritual emphasizes the importance of classroom visits and establishes their importance in improving instruction and learning. Spending just a few hours in the morning with walk-throughs allows you to provide meaningful feedback to teachers, gives you the chance for visibility with students, and lets you stay connected with the learning that is taking place in the classroom.

Learning-Walks Wednesday. Alternate Walk-Through Wednesday with Learning-Walks Wednesday. Plan to meet with teachers and visit other classrooms, providing positive notes and feedback to move learning forward. Establish a specific day each week or month to complete a learning walk. It can be a very rewarding experience for teachers to connect with each other and share ideas and feedback that help them grow as teachers. Planning a regular time allows colleagues to look forward to the event and gives the day a special feeling.

Teamwork Thursday. Establish Thursday as the day where you connect with others. Set up a regular meeting with other administrators around the district who will help you grow as a leader. I often connect with another principal who is just down the street from me. We are able to share ideas, provide each other with support, and answer questions for each other. I feel like we both bring different strengths to the table, and setting up a consistent meeting time allows us to regularly share those strengths with each other. In addition to providing a time for you to connect with other administrators, you can schedule teamwork meetings with teachers to promote collaboration on different projects. In addition, Thursday is the day when we do our staff meetings in our building. Continue the teamwork theme at your staff meetings and promote collaborative discussions.

Good-News-Phone-Call Friday. I enjoy making positive phone calls home to families of students who have had a great week or done something exceptional. It could be a student who had academic success or someone who typically struggles but has a wonderful moment that we want to let parents know about. The good news phone calls usually catch parents off guard. I announce to the parent, "I have John in the office right now. . . and we are making a good news phone call!" Recognizing students on Friday can be a great way to end the week for you, students, and families. You can even add to the theme and recognize staff members by making a good-news phone call home. Calling a colleague's spouse, child, or parent is a great way to recognize staff members for their contributions at your school. What a great way to provide recognition to staff members who go out of their way every day.

Having Nothing Planned (or Planning to Do Nothing)

If you've ever paid close attention to your calendar app, you'll notice an interesting phrase when you don't have anything planned on a specific day. It says: "Nothing planned. Tap to create."

Having blank spaces in your digital or physical calendar can be a bonus. You don't necessarily want to create something to fill the time. Sometimes, you might just need the time to breathe. You might want open spaces in your calendar to absorb all of the fires that constantly arise throughout the day. Or you might leave white space to provide a moment to catch up on your to-do list.

I've always had difficulty with the phrasing of the digital encouragement from my calendar app. You see, there is a big difference between having nothing planned and planning to do nothing. Most of the time, when there is nothing on the calendar, it's because I've intentionally put nothing on the calendar. It's not that there's nothing planned. It's really that I've planned to do nothing.

That's right. I've planned to do nothing.

We honestly fill our schedule beyond capacity at some points. I've had two meetings taking place at the same time and somehow managed to do both. Neither of the meetings had my full attention, but that's what happens when I've scheduled a meeting in the building with a colleague, and then the district schedules an administrative meeting on top of it. It can be downright overwhelming.

The answer to our overscheduling madness is planning to do nothing. Add those empty spaces into your calendar. You can use them to catch up on everything that got swallowed up by the rest of the schedule. You can also use them to do nothing. Open your calendar right now, and add several do-nothing blocks of five or ten minutes each.

Have you done it? OK, how did it feel? I'll bet it felt invigorating. You probably feel like you have more of a spring in your step just by adding those blocks to the calendar.

Just wait until you actually experience one of your do-nothing blocks. If you've been going hard all day long because you've overfilled your calendar, having five minutes to just quietly contemplate can feel amazing.

So if you've got nothing planned somewhere in your calendar, make sure that you truly plan to do nothing.

Preflight Checklist for Mastering Your Time and Energy

- ❏ What strategy from this chapter would you like to try?
- ❏ Why? (your true north)
- ❏ How? (your plan)
- ❏ When? (your timeline)

CONQUERING PROCRASTINATION AND PERFECTIONISM

Procrastination and perfectionism can keep us from doing our best work. If you are anything like me, you can procrastinate with the best of them. I can find ways to procrastinate my procrastination. Yep, I'm that good. I can linger on something for a long time before deciding that I should finally tackle it.

In this section, we will focus on strategies for fighting procrastination, overcoming our tendencies to be perfect, allowing for trade-offs, and examining the single most important piece of technology we own.

Productivity, Motivation, and Procrastination

Why are we so unproductive? Why is it that when we know that a project is due in just two hours, we are spending our time on our phone shopping for the latest haberdashery? Our complete lack of productivity often has only one thing to blame: procrastination. Some of us are complete professionals at procrastination. I like to say that I've earned my black belt in procrastination. I can wait until the last possible minute to get something done and still accomplish my goal. I can find all kinds of other things to occupy my time. Have you ever watched a riveting bowling match or found time to play ping-pong by yourself? Sometimes, both of these options seem better than what you actually should be doing.

Like me, I bet you might be on your way to your procrastination black belt. So how do we fight procrastination? I think our strongest weapons in this battle are establishing routines and creating ways to make procrastination harder. The more friction we can add to the things that waste our time, the stronger we will be in our fight against procrastination. We don't need to be unmotivated and unproductive. Try these strategies for creating friction in the procrastination methods that are killing your productive vibes. Make them work for you.

Install a website blocker or turn off your internet. It can be terrible when the internet goes down at your house because everyone and everything relies so much on being connected. You go over and check the router sixty-five times to figure out when it's back on. Let's take the opposite approach. If you are trying to do something else, turn the router off. Unplug it. Pull a cable. Get done what you need to get done without the distraction of everything online calling your name. There are also several website blocking software options like Freedom or Cold Turkey that might work to keep you from the land of distraction.

Clutter-free and distraction-free workspace. Having a clear workspace can help to eliminate some of the distractions that might derail your timely work. In my office, I have a small round table and a desktop where I may sit to do some of my work. I have a convertible standing desk, which allows me to stand and complete work as well. When I'm working on something, I try to keep my desk as clutter-free as possible. If I'm writing a draft of a parent letter, I'll start at my desk with just a piece of paper and a pen. Nothing else is on the desk to take away from the task at hand. What should be particularly absent from the workspace should be your phone. Try to keep your office clean and tidy, with just enough there to get the job done.

Put a Do Not Disturb sign on your door. Sometimes it's the people that serve as distractions. You might have your office as tidy as can be, your paper and pen in front of you, your door closed, ready to go, and then there's a knock at the door. While you can eliminate all kinds of digital interruptions, it's our colleagues who sometimes keep us from our important work by adding work of their own. The simple answer is to put a Do Not Disturb sign on your door. It can simply say "Do Not Disturb," or you can make an attempt at humor to try to ward people off:

- Do NOT disturb. Concentrating like a cat chasing a laser.
- Do NOT disturb unless you have pizza, ice cream, or there's a massive fire.
- Busy being awesome. Please refrain from opening this door. Seriously, don't do it.

Keeping people at bay can be just as important as everything else that takes away your focus. Do NOT disturb. Just put it out there when you need to get things done.

Lock up your phone. I took my daughter to her first comedy show to see a big-time comedian who was performing new material for the first time in a few years. We went to the show in a fancy theater, and when we got there, we were asked to place our phones in locked bags to keep us from using them. The idea behind this was to keep any video captured from leaking out. It was a simple fix. I immediately wondered about the use of the bag in education. Could we ask kids to put their phones in locked bags every day? Could I get one of these bags to keep me away from my own phone? Whether it's purchasing one of these bags, locking up your phone in a desk drawer, or just leaving it in your car for a while, sometimes you may need to save yourself from barriers to success.

Find a hiding space. In my building, I can be found in my office. If I'm not there, I am quickly reachable via two-way radio: "Mr. Czyz, are you available to come to Room 13?" or "Rich, can you take a phone call?" Being present and visible is a great characteristic for a school administrator to demonstrate—until it comes to productivity. The autopilot way might just be to hide from distractions. If you've tried the Do Not Disturb sign, and people disturb anyway, the best option may be to disappear for a while. Find a nook or cranny in your building, leave your radio in your office (don't worry, they'll page you if it's a true emergency!), and get your stuff done. I won't reveal my hiding place here, because I don't want people to find me. But it's a small room tucked away that many people don't visit very often. It's quiet and allows for fifteen to twenty minutes of pure getting-stuff-done time. If all else fails, just hide from your distractions.

Other Methods for Managing Procrastination

Set up a procrastination jar. Every time you catch yourself procrastinating, put a dollar (or another set amount) into a jar. Give yourself a consequence for all of your procrastinating. You can use the money at the end of the month to treat a colleague or buy dinner for your family. Hopefully, you'll stop postponing your meaningful work when you realize there's a hundred dollars in the jar.

Just start. Sometimes, the hardest part is just starting. Set a timer, and commit to working for just five minutes even if you are not feeling it. Often, you'll be able to continue working past the five-minute mark simply because you started.

Find a buddy. When our kindergarten students need to travel within the building, we like to employ the buddy system. This can work for productivity as well. Find a colleague who also needs to focus on a task. Work in the same space together even if you are working on different tasks. Hopefully, the presence of the other person can help you stay motivated to complete your assignment.

Beat the clock. Set your timer for a short period (15–20 minutes) and sprint to see how much you can accomplish before the timer goes off. The sense of urgency may provide some motivation to power through your tasks quickly.

Establish a productivity playlist. They say music soothes the savage beast. It can also provide the perfect mood for productivity. I have a number of different playlists that I utilize for specific tasks. The Alt-J album *An Awesome Wave* is one of my go-to soundtracks for writing. Bastille's *Bad Blood* is my Friday afternoon favorite. Utilize different playlists to accomplish your pressing tasks.

Shake it up with a change of scenery. We can fall into a trap when we get stuck sitting in the same space trying to complete important tasks. We don't need to associate comfort with procrastination. Instead, find a new space to work. Is there a picnic table outside under a tree that might inspire you to complete your work? How about a standing desk in the hallway away from your office? Changing your scenery can spark productivity. Just find a new spot to work.

Overcoming Perfectionism

The ever-present battle to be perfect is something that can trip up school leaders on a regular basis. We try to do everything a certain way and make sure that everything is just so. I've gotten caught up with my own perfectionist tendencies when I try to write a parent letter. I'll spend an inordinate amount of time writing, revising, sharing it with several staff members for proofreading, and then finally approving a final copy to be sent home. While I don't want to send home any communication to parents with typos, my process can sometimes be too much.

None of us are ever going to be perfect in our roles. There are simply too many decisions, too many responsibilities, and too much that can happen on a day-to-day basis to assume that we will never make mistakes. Sometimes the most productive we can be is to let go of some of those perfectionist tendencies. Try these methods for letting go of perfectionism.

Sometimes, good enough is good enough. If you've been on a plane enough, you know that the landing can be rough. Pilots don't aim for a perfect landing each time, but rather one that is safe and effective. We need to do the same as administrators. Projects and tasks do not need to be flawless, but they need to achieve your primary goals. Think of the example of an email you are crafting to a parent. There are diminishing returns when you work on it for too long. Sometimes, good enough is good enough.

Try setting a timer. If you are working on a task—say, an email to a parent—and have allotted yourself ten minutes for the task, set a timer for eight minutes, and write the email. Once the timer goes off, ask someone to review your email for tone and typos quickly, then hit send on the email. Use your timer to make sure it's good enough.

Accept course correction. You should recognize that many of the projects or tasks you've taken on in the past have not turned out exactly as you initially intended. Sometimes, a project starts in one iteration and turns into something completely different. This is because you were able to course correct along the way. While this seems obvious after the project is completed, it usually doesn't feel that way during the process. We often fight adjustments because of the time, effort, and energy we've already put in. Accept that sometimes we need to course correct, and that failing is not the same as failure. Learn from your mistakes, adjust, and move forward.

To practice, schedule a biweekly or monthly check-in meeting on an ongoing project you are working on. Meet with those involved and find out what's working well and what's not. When challenges come up, and they always do, brainstorm possible solutions and make necessary adjustments to the plan.

Plan with must-haves and nice-to-haves. There are certain things that must happen in order for any task or implementation to be successful. There are also certain outcomes that you would like to see but don't necessarily impact the success of the project. Plan out your assignment with must-haves and nice-to-haves. Readily accept that the assignment is successful if the majority of your must-haves are accomplished, and recognize that any of the nice-to-haves that are accomplished are just gravy. Don't strive to reach an unattainable goal. Accept the wins that you are getting even if you have minor quibbles with how you get them.

Think about an upcoming project you need to work on. Fold a paper in half and label one column "must-haves" and label the other "nice-to-haves." Now list the qualities you absolutely need within the project versus the outcomes that would be beneficial but aren't required. Approach the project with the assumption that you will not have everything on both sides of the list. And that's OK.

Don't sweat the small stuff. There are many times throughout our day that little things come up and don't go our way. I'm guilty of turning these little imperfections into big problems. For example, let's say you are in the middle of a teacher observation when you get called to the office to meet with a facilities representative to talk about an upcoming facilities project. In the past, this type of occurrence would have ruined my day. Now I try to live by the mantra, "This too shall pass." Will this small imperfection matter in five minutes? In an hour? In twenty-four hours? If not, move on and move forward.

Consider setting up a "parking lot" for minor issues. Use a whiteboard or sheet of paper, and list any minor issues that come up during the day. Don't let those minor issues impact the major things you have going on. Add them to your parking lot list and address them all at once later in the week. When you look at the parking lot items, prioritize, delegate, and address them in a calm manner. Issues will arise no matter what, and it's our reaction to them that determines how successful we are in handling them.

Trade-Offs

There are going to be trade-offs. Not everything is going to work out like you wanted it to. You'll have to sacrifice some things that you enjoy, some things that you are nostalgic about because they simply don't make sense anymore. In committing to autopilot, you will make your life easier. You'll make it more efficient. You'll become more productive. But you will have to compromise on certain things. Sometimes, it doesn't matter how something is accomplished, just that it's accomplished. Here are some of the trade-offs that you should learn to be comfortable with:

Lack of control. If you are handing off some of the things on your plate, you are going to have to rely on and trust others to get them done. People that you delegate to may not do things in the exact same manner that you do. That's OK. You should establish trust in others. Know that they will get the job done just as you would've gotten the job done. Just don't fault their methods. Cede control, and cease worrying about those items.

Initial time investment. While automating your processes and implementing autopilot features will start to save more of your time on the back end, it is going to take a large amount of time up front. You'll need to make an initial investment of time. Things will feel uncomfortable at first. You'll want to immediately go back to doing things yourself when you try to delegate an automation task and the person doesn't do it right the first time. Keep at it. It's OK if they don't get it right the first time. Rome wasn't built in a day, and neither will your autopilot improvements happen overnight. Keep with it. Know that any time put out up front will pay dividends in the end.

Quantity versus quality. When you are first automating your processes and trying some of the autopilot strategies, you will tend toward quantity. You'll try to get more done in fewer minutes. When you cross things off of your to-do list because you've automated or delegated, you'll immediately add more, with the idea that emptying things off your list means you can now add more items to it. Try to hold back at adding new items to your list right away. Bask in the changes you make and see how much time you are getting back in your day. Think more about the amount of time you can spend on some of the quality items on your list instead of just adding more of the same low-value tasks that you now have more time for. Just because you have more time doesn't necessarily mean that you now need to do more.

More time-sucks making their presence known. Going on autopilot means you are going to make more time to do the things that you want and need to do. When others see how your schedule has opened up due to delegating and automating, they will try to fill that empty space with other time-sucks. Time-sucks are the things that suck you in (websites, meandering noneducation related conversations, etc.) but add no value to your day. Make sure that saving time does not just give you additional productive time to squander in unproductive ways.

Give Yourself Over to the Idea of Tomorrow

A long-held anecdote claims that Ernest Hemingway would stop his daily writing sessions in the middle of a sentence, even when he had the ability to write more. The idea was that he would know exactly where to begin during his next writing session. I'm not sure whether to believe this about Hemingway's writing, but I've tried the method myself. I don't think the method works for me as a writer, but it teaches us a tremendous lesson about how we approach productivity.

The end of my day usually seems like a blur. Trying to dismiss more than three hundred preschool-through-fifth-grade students always seems like it has its fair share of obstacles. At least once a week, we are dealing with a student who is not sure whether they are a "walker" or a "busser" (a student going home on the bus). Sometimes, the teacher isn't quite sure either, and, on occasion, the parent flat-out doesn't know. After dealing with the stress of a lost or confused student, panicking teacher, and beyond-frantic parent, the last thing I want to do is sit and spend any time with my to-do list. Still, I will often force myself to sit with my list to accomplish some necessary tasks that I didn't get to during the day.

But I get an absolutely magical feeling when I give myself over to the idea of tomorrow. It's a blessing sometimes to look at my list and decide I'll have time to tackle it first thing in the morning. No panic. No guilt. In the morning, it will be waiting exactly where I left it.

What to Do When the Internet Doesn't Work

Have you ever turned on your computer, ready to complete some critical task, only to discover that the internet is down? You will have three options if the internet is not working.

The first is to become upset and frantically refresh your screen every ten seconds until the internet starts working again. This may take you a considerable amount of time and cause a great deal of frustration. I don't recommend this option.

The second option is only available if you use Google Chrome like I do. You'll get the No Internet message along with the little tiny dinosaur right above it. This game was originally built into the Chrome browser to pass the time while you wait for the internet to work again. You can play the game by having the Nointernetasaurus jump over stuff repeatedly. Again, this is a way to pass the time, but I wouldn't recommend this option either.

Instead, your best option is to get up from your computer immediately, and go and do something more productive that doesn't involve the internet. When the No Internet message pops up, it's out of our control. It's almost like a sign that someone is telling you to do something other than sit at your computer waiting for the internet to start back up. Go visit classrooms. Go meet with teachers to discuss some instructional strategies. Go meet with students to find out what they are learning about. Make some good-news phone calls home with students. Read the latest educational journal article you've been meaning to get to. Don't take it personally. Your internet provider is not out to get you, plus you have zero control. Make the time more useful instead.

The Single Most Important Piece of Technology That We Own

Our phones can be one of our biggest distractions. If it's your phone that is distracting you during the workday, there is an easy way to solve your problem. The answer is really very simple, and the key to our freedom from our phones is actually the single most important piece of technology that we own.

Every smartphone has it, and it's the key to reaching all of your wildest dreams. Apple was brilliant enough to include it in its original iPhone design and continues to make it an integral part of the design all the way through the current iteration. Samsung sells its phones with this feature as well. Google included it on the first Pixel phone too.

This single feature will help you with your productivity. It will help to improve your relationships with others around you. It will help you to get more sleep and be a better partner, parent, colleague, and friend. Some people have only used this feature once, and some haven't used it in a long time.

I know. I know. The suspense is killing you. Let's examine this most important piece of technology together. Pull out your phone. I know it's probably in your pocket or sitting on the table next to you. Maybe you are actually reading this book on your phone right now. I'm sure that whatever phone you have features this all-important technology.

OK, so the single most important piece of technology we own is… (drum roll please!!!)

. . . the off button on our phones.

That's right, the answer to all of our prayers is right there on the side of the phone. Want your time back? Want to get more done? Want to engage in your creative passions? The answer to all of this is very simple. Shut off your phone. I wanted to make this section of the book longer with more information, but it was so blatantly obvious that I could only capture the message in a single sentence.

Turn off your damn phone!

Why You Need a Phone Jail

It started as a joke with my family. I had been discussing a family member who is attached to their phone. My dad proudly waltzed into my house a few days later proclaiming, "We bought you a phone jail!" I had no idea what my dad was talking about, but he soon produced a box that had a very loud font on the side labeled "phone lockup." It was exactly as described: a small wooden platform with slots for smartphones, surrounded by a metal cage with a locking door (lock and key included). It seemed like it was meant to be a gag gift, but it actually came in handy in our household with three phone-owning children and two phone-owning adults. We quickly implemented a rule: All phones in the phone jail when we go to bed. Dinnertime was also a major phone-jail time. Most of the time, we didn't even lock the phone jail. It was just enough of a reminder to everyone that there should be some sacred time when we are not using our phones.

If you want to be truly productive as a school administrator, I suggest the purchase of a phone jail. I've seen some really expensive ones online and some similar to the one I have for about ten dollars. You can put one on your desk and lock up your phone when you are trying to remain focused on a single task. If you are hosting a meeting, you can serve as a role model and place your phone in the lockup to demonstrate your commitment to the meeting. While you can actually lock up the phone and give the key to someone else for safekeeping, you can also just use the jail as a symbolic gesture. Just putting your phone inside the jail can help you to convince yourself that you should be working on something more important, rather than being distracted by your phone.

Preflight Checklist for Conquering Procrastination and Perfectionism

- ❏ What strategy from this chapter would you like to try?
- ❏ Why? (your true north)
- ❏ How? (your plan)
- ❏ When? (your timeline)

AUTOMATION, DELEGATION, AND EMPOWERMENT

In the last chapter, we learned that procrastination can really destroy what we are trying to accomplish and that accepting some trade-offs in order to be more productive is just part of the deal. We can absolutely get more done when we let go of some things, utilizing technology and delegating to others to help us accomplish our goals. In this chapter, we will find out what's better than multitasking, learn how to delegate our work, and discover automation strategies for staff absences, classroom walk-throughs, and student discipline.

Multitasking Versus Multi-Asking

The term *multitasking* was introduced at some point in the 1960s to describe a computer being able to perform multiple functions at the same time. It wasn't until the 1990s that the word was popularized to describe humans being able to perform multiple functions at the same time. If you look up *multitasking* online, you'll find a variety of research both praising and condemning the practice.

Early on, I thought that I was more productive when I was multitasking. I would start a project, transition to something else that popped up, switch to answering several emails, and then move back to the original task. It would take me several hours to get through the three or four tasks on my list. In the end, I would feel accomplished because I had completed a few of the tasks that needed to be completed.

Over time, I figured out that a lot of the tasks that I was completing by multitasking were administrivia. It looked as if I was finishing and completing things, but they were really trivial, uninteresting, and time-consuming tasks. I learned that by trying to complete everything on my list at once, I really wasn't achieving anything meaningful. While it wasn't sudden, I gradually shifted away from the multitasking mindset and changed paths completely. Instead of multitasking, I started to believe in the philosophy of multi-asking.

The idea behind multi-asking is that instead of taking everything on yourself, you need to rely on others to help you, especially with some of the minutiae. While other staff members including office staff, teachers, custodians, and school counselors are willing and often better equipped to handle certain tasks, you as the school leader simply need to ask them to help. While others can help with some of the mundane tasks that we face each day, even more of these asks can be accomplished through automation strategies. You can even turn over some tasks to students to help empower them to take on more responsibility within your school setting.

Think about how much of your daily to-do list actually needs to be done by you. Think about how much of it could more successfully be turned over to others. Let's explore a few examples.

Each month, our school hosts student awards. Teachers present certificates to students and say several nice words about them while the rest of the student body watches and cheers on their classmates. It's a wonderful way to recognize students who have been successful and are trying really hard. At the end of our student awards assemblies, we take photos of all of the winners by class. In the past, I would be the one with the school iPad taking pictures of each group of students. Taking photos of each class would take about twenty minutes or so. I've learned that it's actually better to assign this role to students. They generally are better at taking pictures than I am, anyway. When they are finished they share them with our school secretary, and she prints them so that they can be posted on a bulletin board in our main hallway. What would have taken me forty to sixty minutes to accomplish only takes a handful of people a few minutes each.

Multi-asking gives you the opportunity to take things off of your plate while recognizing and taking advantage of the strengths of those that work around you.

Delegate and Elevate

I've just suggested a form of delegating. I want you to multi-ask more often than you multitask. In order to do this, you need to trust those around you. You're going to want to rely on others to use their expertise to get things done.

If you've gotten into school administration to prove how smart you are or to exert your expertise over all of your colleagues, I would say you've gotten it wrong. Delegating gives you the opportunity to put trust in those around you. There is an interesting side effect that comes with trusting others and multi-asking. As you begin to rely on others and build trust in them, not only are you going to delegate to them, you are also going to elevate them as well. The more you trust people to help you, the more that they will actually be able to help you.

When you delegate, you will elevate people. You'll develop trust in them, and they'll begin to demonstrate leadership skills of their own. Maybe they will leave you to take on a school administrative role of their own. And that is one of the best things that can happen. You may think to yourself, *If this person leaves, then who will take on their responsibilities that I've delegated to them?* But this is exactly what you want. Once somebody leaves, you can work to delegate and elevate someone else. The beautiful thing about working with others to take on shared tasks is that you'll build new leaders by helping others to discover their own leadership skills.

Customer Support Tickets

After my role as a classroom teacher for several years, I was transferred into a position as an instructional technology coach. My job duties included working closely with teachers to help them introduce new instructional strategies and new technologies into the classroom. In this role, I worked closely with our district's technology department, and I learned a newfound respect for what they do on a regular basis.

Most technology departments manage their workload through an online system that tracks work tickets. If a staff member is having an issue with some form of technology (their interactive whiteboard isn't working, they are locked out of their email, their printer won't work, etc.), they register the problem online, and district technicians pick up the tickets in order to address the problems. While there are many different software platforms for tracking work tickets, the idea is the same in most schools and districts.

This sort of system allows for the process to be automated. Technicians can log in to the system, see what needs to be addressed, fix the problem, and close out the ticket when finished. The system keeps track of the work that the technicians are doing and ensures that all issues are addressed. I think this is the biggest benefit of such a system. Having worked in school districts that do not have such a system for technology issues (or issues in facilities or maintenance), I know that problems can often be forgotten or overlooked before someone is actually addressing them.

At the time of school closures during the pandemic, I needed a way to check in on teachers and make sure they had everything they needed to be able to do their job. Inspired by the tech ticket system, I developed a system of customer support tickets to ensure that I was meeting the needs of teachers who were in a wholly unique situation. Using a simple online survey form (Google Forms), I had teachers fill out the form if they needed something or if they had a specific question. The information was then tracked to an online spreadsheet. While I had access to the spreadsheet and addressed any specific needs or questions, I also shared access to the sheet with our office secretaries, who were often able to answer a question before I was able to. On the spreadsheet, we would record our name next to a question/need that we had handled, and we were able to track what had been completed or still needed to be finished. Our customer support ticket system was born.

I've used similar online forms and spreadsheets to track other specific needs such as end-of-year room maintenance or beginning-of-the-year requests.

While there are many specific software programs that can be utilized to manage customer support tickets, you can also set up a simple Google Form or even a spreadsheet. When teachers email with a request, you add the "ticket" to your spreadsheet, and check it off as you finish it. Whether you are utilizing software, a Google Form/spreadsheet, or even something rudimentary like a notebook or sticky notes, developing a system of customer support tickets can help you to ensure that every task gets done, and that no one is duplicating efforts.

Your Problem or Theirs?

How do you remain calm, cool, and collected amid all of the busyness surrounding you? One of the things that makes me a good leader is my ability to remain calm during times of crisis and uproar. During more than one emergency situation at school, I've had a colleague share that my calm demeanor was refreshing in a difficult moment.

I've always liked to describe myself as even-keeled. I try not to let myself get too low or too high in response to a given situation. One of my favorite sayings is, "It's never as good as it feels, and it's never as bad as it seems."

This mentality has helped me to maintain my productivity amid even the most difficult situations. I try not to let others' emotions surrounding their issues upset my productivity. Another quote here sticks out: "Failure to adequately plan on your part does not constitute a crisis on my part." How often do you have someone coming to you at the last minute with something that suddenly needs to be done? While you may have your tasks in order, suddenly you are bombarded by someone else's something that suddenly needs to become your something. There are several ways to handle these types of situations. Some are more harsh than others, but you can use any of them to combat someone else's problem that suddenly becomes yours.

Don't make it your problem (at least right away!). Use the quote above to show someone that their failure to plan means that you are not going to address their problem right away. Place dealing with their issue on an open space within your schedule when it is convenient for you. This is especially helpful if it is a person who is a repeat offender and constantly brings you their problems at the last minute.

Guide the person in solving their own problem. Explain to the person how their problem can be solved and what they will need to do in order to solve it. This type of explanation usually lets the person know that they really should not be coming to you at the last minute with their problem. Do it in a nice way, and provide several options for how they can solve their own problem. This should be the last time that you face last-minute problems from them.

Help the person while communicating your boundaries. Let the person know that you appreciate the pickle that they are in, but it helps everyone involved when some planning is done to avoid these situations. Offer to help them in this situation but remind them that, in the future, they should put forth more effort in planning ahead to be more efficient.

No matter which approach you take to help the person in these types of situations, remind the person that your time is valuable. A simple email can be sent with a gentle reminder: "Thank you for bringing issue X to my attention. While it is important that we address this at this time, please remember that adequate planning can help avoid these last-minute crises. Let's work to address this situation now, and let's meet afterward to discuss how we can avoid similar situations in the future."

People will constantly try to turn their problems into your problems. It's important to set boundaries for yourself, and let others know when they have crossed those boundaries.

Try these tips for establishing solid boundaries as well:

Explicitly state your boundaries. It's OK to let people know what you will and won't do. A message at the bottom of your emails that states your boundaries serves as the perfect reminder and models for others how boundaries can be established. You can set several different responses depending on the situation:

- "I strive to protect my family time at home. As such, I typically check emails between 8:00 a.m. and 4:30 p.m. Monday through Friday. If this is an urgent matter, please call me directly."
- "Thank you for your email. I will check and respond to emails during the workweek within 24 hours."
- "To ensure focused work, I only check email once a day. You can expect a response within 24 hours."
- "I do not respond to emails outside of the school day (8:00 a.m. to 4:30 p.m., Monday through Friday). I will begin responding to emails again tomorrow morning."
- "To preserve personal time, I do not check emails over the weekend. I will begin responding to emails during school hours on Monday. Thank you for your understanding."

- "In order to maintain productivity, I only check email at two specific times during the day. I will get back to you as soon as possible within these windows. If you require immediate assistance, please contact the main office directly."
- "Thank you for your email. I try to respond to all emails within 24 hours. Please contact the main office with any urgent needs. Thank you for your patience."

Keep your boundaries positive. People will accept your boundaries when they know that you are committed to helping them. You can positively state your boundary by saying something like, "While I'm not able to meet in the morning before 8:30, I will be available anytime in the morning between 9:30 and 10:30 or in the afternoons from 1:30 to 2:30." If you can establish clear-cut boundaries while also providing help to those that need it, everyone will appreciate your boundaries.

Recognize the boundaries of everyone else. You can't be the only one with boundaries. You will also need to respect the boundaries of others. You can't ask people not to email you after four thirty but then send emails at ten, just as your colleagues are getting ready for bed. If you want colleagues to respect your boundaries, you have to set an example to follow. Respect your colleagues and their time. There is no other way.

Respectfully decline. I've always been the administrator to say yes to teachers. I'm of the mindset that if a teacher is excited about something, and they bring it to me with a request, I should say yes. Number one, I don't want to dampen that excitement; number two, if it is something that might benefit our students, why would I say no? However, there are some requests that we simply can't accommodate. In those situations, politely decline. "I'm sorry that we can't take this project on in its current state. Maybe we can talk about some changes that would allow us to do something like this." Be up front with people instead of stringing them along with a maybe. Let them know why you can't do something, and offer some alternatives if possible.

Stay firm and seek compromise. Don't bend to your colleagues' will when it comes to your boundaries. There is a reason why you set them in the first place. Stay firm and resolute, and try to seek compromise that respects your boundaries while also trying to accommodate the needs of your colleagues. They will respect you more for setting boundaries and sticking to them.

> **CONTROL PANEL CHECK: AUTOSAVE ATTACHMENTS**
>
> Have you ever spent more than twenty minutes desperately searching for that attachment that you just know someone sent you maybe last month? Or maybe it was the month before? They did send you the attachment, right? Did you download it? This can be a frustrating exercise in futility, especially when you realize that you didn't download it, and therefore need to go back to the original email.
>
> No more. You need to autosave attachments. Within most email providers, you can find an automation setting to autosave any attachments that are sent to you via email. There are also other apps that can accomplish the same thing for you. You'll now have one folder to go to and find exactly what it is that you've been looking for.
>
> Get those attachments saved automatically. You are a sophisticated, productive human being. Save yourself time from searching like a madman!

Dealing with Staff Absences

Why do you feel overwhelmed when you wake up in the morning? For me, it starts with checking the absentee report for the day and trying to figure out who's absent, which classes have to be covered, and which staff members are available to cover. It's stressful. I know that students will be off-kilter with a substitute in their classroom. I know that those other staff members who I might pull from their regular responsibilities to cover a class won't be happy. And if I don't have coverage, then I have to split up classes and send the students to any number of other teachers in the building. No wonder it's overwhelming.

Every morning when faced with this dilemma, I would always imagine that there had to be a better way. How could it be easier? I started with a simple premise. The two teachers I relied on most to cover classes were the basic skills teachers. We were able to cancel their classes if they had to cover another teacher's class. I decided to take the guesswork and thinking out of the equation. I spoke with both teachers, and we decided that for any teacher out in grades kindergarten through second grade, one teacher would handle the absence. Then for any teacher out in grades three through five, the other teacher would handle the absence.

While this strategy didn't really solve the main problem of teachers being absent, it at least made it a little easier to deal with. Some other strategies that might help with the substitute shortage are below.

Digital substitute plans. Maintain a bank of emergency substitute plans from each teacher in a digital folder that all substitute teachers and staff fill-ins have access to.

Schedule of available subs. Maintain a chart that shows which teachers are available to cover during certain periods of the day. This way, you don't need to think about who can cover a class in a pinch. Just go to the chart and find your hero.

Create a substitute handbook. This manual should feature general lesson plan ideas for multiple grade levels, essential information about your school, school policies, classroom management strategies, and emergency procedures.

Utilize prerecorded lessons. Have teachers create video lessons to share with classes in their absence. I once worked with an art teacher who was assigned to jury duty every Thursday for nearly twenty weeks.

He ended up missing the same five classes each week. We filmed all of his lessons ahead of time, and a sub just showed the videos each week.

Maintain an open learning library. Utilize the library to host multiple classes at once when more than one teacher is out with no sub. Students can work on open learning plans or project-based learning while also completing independent study under the watchful eye of a few staff members.

> ### Substitutes Should Be Treated Like Royalty
>
> We all know that good subs are hard to come by. This is why we should be treating all of our willing substitutes like royalty in our buildings. Kings and queens. Princesses and princes. Everyone who steps foot into one of our buildings should get the red carpet rolled out for them.
>
> I've already shared a few logistical strategies for making it easier to obtain and maintain substitutes, which can lead to more productive schools. Utilizing handbooks, digital resources, emergency lesson plans, and more can make it easier on those that keep the school running in the absence of regular staff. There are also other strategies you can use to appeal to guest teachers in your building and keep them coming back. While you may spend some extra time and effort with some of these strategies, it will be worth it when you get quality substitutes joining your staff on a regular basis to take care of your students. Never forget: Subs are people too!
>
> *Strike the "sub" title.* When have you ever heard anyone speak positively about a substitute teacher before? The two words strike fear in the heart of an educator and inspire students everywhere to misbehave in ways that haven't even been invented yet. The title *substitute* is boring. It conveys someone who is there to babysit and not be invested in the students. Even worse is the title *permanent substitute*. Let's

instead honor those walking into our classrooms to do more than just fill in. *Guest educator* has a certain ring to it. So does *visiting teacher*. More of a fan of *guest instructor* or *interim instructor*? How about *guest learning facilitator*? Just find a title that bestows a little more respect on those brave enough to enter our classrooms and those willing to commit to students when others can't.

Meet and greet. I know the morning can be one of the craziest times of the day in a school. You are running around trying to cover all of your classes, and you only have one guest educator coming in to cover a class for the day. It is so important to greet that person as they come into your building: "Good morning! Welcome to our school. Thank you for joining us as a guest educator today. We are so happy you are with us. Let me show you to your classroom." Make sure that each visiting teacher feels welcome, and, more importantly, wants to come back.

Flow and show. You've greeted your guest instructor, and you've shown them to their room for the day. Also make sure you provide an easy-to-follow map of your school. I'm not talking about the one that was originally created in 1973 and has been photocopied sixty-seven different times. Create a colorful map (flow) with easy-to-read names and class numbers. Also include the names and room numbers of some helpful people. This helps your guest to find their way and to find help when they get stuck. Also be sure to provide your guest with a detailed schedule (show) for their day. If they are going to cover multiple classes during the day or need to cover classes during meetings, be sure to outline each teacher that they will stand in for, and make clear where they should be at specific times. Providing a color-coded map and schedule needs to be step one.

> *Check in.* I know. You've got a lot to do. But do you want that visiting instructor to come back? Of course you do. Check in on your guests several times throughout the day: "How's it going? Is there anything that you need? Do you need to take a restroom break while I visit with the class?" This will also help you to know which visiting teachers you'd like to come back, and which you feel would be better off visiting somewhere else. Checking in will help you to figure out who you can consistently rely on.
>
> *Celebrate your interim instructors.* I know of another school principal who hosts an annual luncheon for all of the visiting teachers who have worked in the building for the year. It's an incredible gesture, and it speaks to how visiting teachers are valued and treated within that building. You can bet that this building is able to retain guest educators more than other buildings in the area. Maybe a luncheon is not necessary, but how about handing them a care package as they walk through the door? A cold water bottle? Some fun size candy? A stress ball with your school logo on it? Celebrating your visitors goes a long way. Help them to help you.
>
> While some of these activities will take up more of your time, they will also help you to retain quality people. Subs are people too! Put the effort in to ensure that your guest teachers feel welcome and want to return. It will be well worth the time and effort.

Dealing with Discipline

If you are a building administrator (especially at the middle- or high-school level), much of your day may be tied up dealing with student discipline issues. Even though I have spent my administrative career working at the elementary level, I feel like student discipline takes up a supersize portion of my day. There are so many steps involved in a single discipline issue:

- talking with the student(s) involved
- speaking with the teacher to find out exactly what happened (after not getting the truth from the student)
- talking with the student(s) again
- communicating with parents
- sharing the consequences with the student and teacher
- documenting all of these steps

It can be an incredibly time-consuming part of our day to deal with a single incident. Keep in mind that we are usually facing several incidents a day, and I often find that I will arrive in the office to find multiple issues waiting for me at once. There has to be a way to streamline this process and still involve everyone that needs to be involved.

Over the years, I've developed a system that helps me handle discipline issues while minimizing the time involved in the process. It's really very basic, and some of you may utilize a similar system. Please note that, like you, I've tried several different strategies for dealing with office referrals and handling discipline in an efficient manner. Over time, I eventually settled on a system that keeps everyone in the loop and requires minimal input in terms of effort while still maintaining some sort of efficiency.

Let me walk you through the steps of my current discipline workflow:

1. A staff member reports a discipline issue involving a student, either in person or by email.
2. I speak with the student to investigate the issue. I follow up with other students, if necessary.
3. I document the discipline issue in my notebook, including conversation notes and any supporting evidence.
4. If warranted, I communicate a consequence to the student.

5. Once addressed, I will email (for less severe infractions) or place a phone call to the parent (more serious issues), detailing the incident, consequence, and any other relevant information. If making a phone call, I will always follow up with a detailed email.
6. Any email sent to a parent is also copied to the classroom teacher, our main office secretary, and our school counselor.
7. The incident is documented in our student management system by the secretary, who also files a paper copy in a discipline binder.
8. I follow up with any additional parent correspondence and update records as needed.

The beauty of this system is that all stakeholders are involved throughout the communication portion. When the email is sent to the parent and teacher and recorded by the secretary, there is no need to have a separate conversation with the teacher. If the teacher has questions about the consequence or any additional questions, I encourage them to follow up with me.

So the overarching workflow looks like this:

1. Talk to student(s).
2. Email parent (include teacher and secretary).
3. Follow up on any questions.

Part of the reason this has been a successful approach to discipline is that the communication piece is automated. Once the parent knows (via email), the teacher knows, and the record keeper knows exactly what to record in the student management system. It helps to remove the school administrator from some of the steps that usually bog them down.

It's not a perfect system by any means. As the administrator, you still need to meet with and question students, and often this is the work that ties you up. It does, however, remove some of the tedious communication and notification steps. The most important part of student discipline is often the conversations you have with students to find out the underlying issue behind any discipline infractions, and the communication you have with them about how they can try a different approach in the future. Streamlining the parent communication and automating the record-keeping portion is made easy by documenting everything clearly in the email, while also copying all of the relevant parties involved.

Automated Walk-Through Feedback

As an instructional leader in a school, I always want to be present in classrooms to see what instruction and learning looks like. When I first started as a building principal, I would try to get into every classroom every day and share consistent feedback with teachers. I quickly found that, along with other responsibilities, it's tough to visit each classroom daily for an instructional round to provide feedback. I settled on hitting up several classrooms per day, and trying to share feedback with the teacher. On good days, I would visit the classroom, stay for five or six minutes, and leave a sticky note with some positive or critical feedback for the teacher.

On some occasions, I'd be radioed out of the classroom and think about what feedback I wanted to share as I hurriedly exited the room to return to the main office. After dealing with the fire, and other normal parts of the day, I'd eventually see the teacher in the hallway three hours later, and whatever brilliant nugget I was going to share with them was suddenly gone and nowhere to be found. It would happen to me all the time. I would have really meaningful feedback to share but forget exactly what I wanted to say.

What was I going to do to fix this? You guessed it! I wanted to automate the system to achieve the following goals:

- be able to share feedback with the teachers immediately upon leaving the classroom
- gather the data I was gathering from each of the classroom visits

I worked through several versions of my system before I landed on something that worked. I created a Google Form that had a dropdown menu for each teacher. It also had a comment box where I would share specific feedback. I set up the form to automatically ship a copy of the form response (and feedback) to my inbox. From there, I would forward the feedback to the teacher.

The beauty in this system was that all of the feedback I entered into the form during each walk-through would be saved in a spreadsheet. Trends and patterns quickly emerged as I looked at all of the walk-through feedback. I was also able to track how often I visited each classroom and whether I'd missed any specific classrooms during weekly visits. Automation of my walk-throughs, even with this minimalist approach, allowed me to streamline my classroom visits. In an hour, I was able to hit several classrooms and provide each teacher with feedback about the time I was in the classroom. The feedback I leave typically comes in three varieties:

Positive feedback. "I loved the way that students were engaged in creating their own questions about what they want to learn as you approach the new science unit. Thank you for letting me visit your classroom!"

Critical feedback. "Thanks for letting me visit today! I noticed that the questions being asked during the whole group lesson were low-level fact questions. Are you also incorporating higher-level questioning during this unit? I'll share a great question matrix that might help."

Resources. "I loved that students were so engaged during the lesson on the Macy's Thanksgiving Day Parade today! Have you read the book *Balloons Over Broadway* with the students? It's a great picture book that can also be enhanced with a project-based approach in which students create their own balloon parade. Maybe something to consider?"

Each of these might take thirty seconds to a minute to share as I leave the classroom. At the end of the month, I can review the classroom walk-through data and determine what teachers might need help with. Let's say I'd hit several classrooms where low-level questions were common. I might share some questioning techniques and strategies at our next staff meeting to help with this process.

To recap this process:

1. Google Form feedback.
2. Email to self.
3. Forward email to teachers.
4. Review data.

Other systems may work for you in a similar fashion. Maybe you keep a notebook where you record all of your data, including dates, times, subject area, and feedback. After documenting in your notebook, you might then leave a sticky note or email the teachers when you return to your office. However, the digital system seems to be a more obvious choice because you can easily record information about each classroom visit. Another positive to using the digital form is that other evaluators, such as district curriculum supervisors or other administrators, can utilize the same document to add feedback for the teacher as well.

If you haven't already automated your walk-through process, now may be the time to consider it.

Who's the Instructional Leader, Anyway?

My journey to the role of principal took some unique turns. I actually served in a director of curriculum role before I became a principal. Because of my previous experience as a director, I prioritize the role of principal as instructional leader. Even though it's difficult to manage roles as both a manager and instructional leader, I think it can be done. There has to be a balance between the management and logistics of the building and the instructional program taking place at the school.

One of the reasons to try to delegate and automate is to find more time to be that instructional leader within the building. Look at these ideas to infuse some more instructional leadership throughout your day.

Classroom visits. Implement a daily system where you visit classrooms on a regular basis. Schedule a specific time each day and visit several classrooms at a particular grade level or within a department. In order to maintain efficiency, set a silent timer on your phone for five to seven minutes. Once the timer goes off, go visit another class. Combine this with a system for feedback. You can keep feedback as simple as a sticky note dropped on the teachers desk when you leave or implement a digital system like the automated walk-through feedback mentioned previously. The key is to maintain a strict schedule and be consistent in how often you visit classrooms. In a thirty-minute period, you can visit three or four classrooms each day and provide meaningful feedback to those teachers.

Weekly "Coffee and Curriculum" chat. Meaningful conversation does not need to come from a formal professional development session. Schedule a weekly chat where you buy the coffee and invite colleagues to join you to discuss an aspect of the curriculum. It can be as quick as fifteen minutes but probably doesn't need to be more than a half hour. Set a topic and let colleagues discuss or keep it an open format for ideas, questions, and discussion. Just gather those interested and promote positive conversation in a short period of time. One rule: Remain positive. No grumbling, complaining, or whining!

Keep it organized. If you are sharing instructional information with teachers, keep it in one place. Whether it's a Google Classroom, a shared Slack, or a digital folder, keep all of the information in one place for teachers to review. I share a weekly Friday Focus through Smore digital newsletters that houses all of the instructional information I want to share with teachers. I'll include links to different instructional strategies or model videos, as well as any new curriculum updates. Teachers can always go back to the weekly newsletters to find any of the information. The organization piece is key. Sending an email one week, a link to a Google Classroom the next week, and following up with a hard copy of the latest curriculum updates only confuses teachers. They have no idea where they saw that one thing that can help them, and they end up coming back to you to ask where to find it. Save them (and yourself) some time. Keep it in one location!

Host a focused learning walk. Again, the key to being productive about instructional leadership is focusing your time. Meet every other week or monthly with teachers to conduct a twenty-minute learning walk through classrooms. This can happen before or after school or during a prep period. Give each teacher a stack of sticky notes and silently walk through specific classrooms. Teachers can write one thing that they love from the classroom on one sticky note and provide a specific piece of feedback on another sticky note. Each teacher leaves their two sticky notes for the classroom teacher, and everyone gains some valuable feedback about their classroom. In twenty minutes, you are providing a meaningful forum for instructional improvement.

Strict scheduling of meetings. Human beings love routines. They love knowing what's coming next. No matter what instructional planning or meeting you host, keep a strict schedule of these meetings. I send out a calendar in August that outlines all of our meetings for the year: monthly staff meetings, monthly curriculum meetings, professional development sessions, data team meetings, intervention service meetings, etc. Every meeting has a particular day. Staff meetings are the first Thursday of the month. Data meetings take place on Tuesdays. Monthly curriculum meetings are the second Thursday of each month. Intervention meetings happen on Wednesdays. This type of schedule, sent ahead of time, allows teachers to know exactly what's coming. There are no surprises, and the early notification allows everyone involved to stay organized.

Establish an instructional challenge. Having a themed instructional challenge can help colleagues to engage in instructional improvement. One of the ways I engaged in writing this book was participating in a summer writing challenge dubbed the #1000WordsOfSummer on social media. I managed to write one thousand words each day for more than a month. It inspired me and kept me accountable. You can do a similar instructional challenge. Ask writing teachers to write five hundred words each day for a month. This will help give them better insight into their students' writing practice. Better yet, ask nonwriting teachers to do the same thing. This gives them critical insight into how students process writing. Ten-, twenty-, and thirty-day challenges can keep teachers engaged and inspired and encourage collaboration and camaraderie within the building.

Instructional time audits. In order to be productive, we sometimes need to take a step back and look at how we are actually using our time. Some teachers, when they get into a regular routine, don't realize how they are utilizing their time in the classroom. When I'm in an observation with a teacher and their opening minilesson (which is supposed to be ten minutes) actually lasts twenty-seven minutes, it always sparks an eye-opening conversation. Encourage teachers to conduct a time audit of their instructional minutes. How much of the seventy-minute math block is actually dedicated to instruction and learning? Is there any wasted time? Can something be eliminated? Teachers start by documenting how the minutes are actually used. They can write down the minutes themselves, ask a colleague to do it, or even involve a student. Once the minutes are recorded, the teacher can look at the list to determine if the instructional minutes are being best utilized or if there are different ways to be more productive and efficient. Recording how you are using your allotted time can provide a keen insight into what instruction and learning looks like in the classroom.

> **CONTROL PANEL CHECK: AUTO TABS**
>
> You open up your computer first thing in the morning and check your daily staff attendance. You open your district email. You check the weather forecast for the day. You bring up the building cameras on an online server. There are probably nine more websites that you have to visit each day as well. If you don't have all of these websites set to automatically open on your computer each morning, you are definitely doing something wrong. By the time you open up each of the websites manually, you are ten minutes into your day. Ten minutes that you don't have.
>
> Set up your computer to automatically open all of the tabs that you need. It'll save a lot of time. It will keep you informed about everything you need to know, and you will always be prepared.

Preflight Checklist for Automation, Delegation, and Empowerment

- [ ] What strategy from this chapter would you like to try?
- [ ] Why? (your true north)
- [ ] How? (your plan)
- [ ] When? (your timeline)

STREAMLINING YOUR WORKFLOWS

A *workflow* is the process by which you start and finish an administrative task. Some of your workflows are probably organized and efficient while some may need work. You'll also find that many distractions often interrupt your workflows. In this part of the book, we will visit with our old friend elimination, learn about the power of checklists, keep an organized notebook, and find out how scripts can help us.

Your Old Friend, Elimination

When I go to promote this book on a podcast and the interviewer asks, "What is the one autopilot strategy that you think will most help people?" I'm going to point to this section of the book. Even if you as the reader take nothing else from the book, I hope that you will at least be able to apply the next principle to your own role as an educator.

It can be hard to let go of things. There are the traditions, practices, and habits that we've always maintained. We hold onto nostalgia and celebrate rituals that don't really make any sense in today's world. We are sometimes trapped by menial tasks of our own choosing. There is a lot on our to-do list that we do just because it's there. We really need to look at our tasks critically and decide if absolutely everything is necessary.

Many of the traditions and practices that we hold onto are like old friends:

"Staff meetings have always been there when I needed them," you tell yourself. "The monthly newsletter has been by my side since we were in grade school," you'll say to no one in particular. "The emergency sub plan binders have been my rock through thick and thin," you will say to your colleagues as they roll their eyes.

Recognizing the traditional practices that you need to get rid of can be exactly like suddenly realizing that the old friend you've been relying on since you were thirteen maybe isn't the best influence on your life. There is one old friend, though, who you haven't talked to in a while, and you may just need to give him a call. That old friend is elimination.

Elimination is the old friend that always helps us get through tough times. Elimination can be there when our traditions and rituals aren't working for us anymore. So, if there is one thing you should do right now, it's give elimination a call.

Create a list of everything that you currently do as an administrator. As you look down at your list, I want you to look at each item and ask two simple questions:

1. Does this task have any value?
2. Does this task help me accomplish my goals?

Let's examine the questions more carefully. First, the value question: How important is this task to you? If something is high value, the tasks stay, but low-value tasks may be moved down or eliminated from your list. Avoid tasks that don't benefit you. And now, the second question: Does this task help accomplish your goals? The key word here is *your*. If a task doesn't help you accomplish your goals, eliminate it. Don't waste time on others' goals at the expense of your own.

So ask yourself the two questions and if you answer with a flat-out no to either question, you should probably eliminate it from your list. Don't let the nostalgia that you feel for that item keep it on the list. Try to pare down your responsibilities by eliminating. The elimination of certain items will help you to become much more productive.

Elimination can be your best friend. You just have to learn to do it more often. When in doubt, throw it out.

Eliminate Decisions

Former President Barack Obama said, "You'll see I wear only gray or blue suits. I'm trying to pare down decisions. I don't want to make decisions about what I'm eating or wearing. Because I have too many other decisions to make."

All of us as educators should consider this insight. We do face way too many decisions. And sometimes we can reach paralysis by analysis and struggle to make a decision because of all of the ramifications. We need to eliminate inconsequential decisions where we can.

I've taken a page from the former president's book in terms of decision-making about what to wear. I'm the proud principal of Yardville Elementary, home of the Yardville Stars. A few years ago, a parent from our school redesigned our school logo and created an amazing, modern brand for our school. When the spirit-wear order came up, I ordered four pullovers in different colors with the logo on them. I proudly represent the Yardville Stars each day and don't have to worry about what I'm wearing. It eliminates several decisions each morning: What color shirt? What color tie? Do I have to iron? It is quite easy to pair the pullovers with a pair of khaki pants and my shoes, and I have a uniform each day. They look professional and eliminate more decisions before I even get into work. Of course, I wear a shirt and tie (and jacket) on special occasions, but otherwise, I'm repping the Yardville Stars!

How can you eliminate decisions that are time-consuming and create more stress? Try the following strategies for eliminating decisions.

Start with the dress code. I was talking to a teacher the other day about my choice to wear the Yardville Stars pullover. She was bemoaning the fact that she had to wake up every day and think about what she was going to wear and how much easier it was for me. She said the magic words: "I wish I could just wear a Yardville polo shirt each day." My simple response was, "You can." This solved a dilemma for her and made the morning less stressful. Give everyone the choice to wear branded uniforms that look professional and cause a little less anxiety over deciding what they need to wear each day.

Establish trust and delegate those decisions. There are a lot of tiny decisions that come up during the day that swallow our time and energy. There are also many other leaders in the building who want to help with those decisions. It is your responsibility to create other leaders (whether staff or students) where you can establish trust and let others help you. I'll share a specific example. It's always great when a school shares a ton of pictures and information on its social media accounts. However, this can be very time-consuming. Taking pictures or having them sent to you, downloading them, changing formats, and posting to a variety of social media outlets can be a full-time job. Instead of doing it yourself, delegate and hire a trusted social media manager. I'm not talking about paying someone else to do the job, but about leaving it up to students. In my previous school, I let a few of our students loose with an iPad and had them take pictures to share on our school social media account. I showed them how to post, and ensured the pictures were a good representation of our school. After a few weeks of training, the students were ready to run with it. They actually captured better pictures than I would have. Students can even use AI to help shorten messages into 140 characters. It's a win-win.

Create or utilize if-then scenarios. It can help to think through decisions before they need to be decided. Considering several if-then scenarios can help you to make better decisions in the moment. *If* this happens, *then* I will respond in this way. A perfect example is the use of a code of conduct for handling discipline issues. The code of conduct outlines a number of infractions that students might commit, with varying degrees of accountability and varying consequences. By consistently relying upon the code of conduct, you can eliminate decisions that have already been made for you. *If* a student is using inappropriate language in the lunchroom, *then* they will eat in the main office with me where we will have a conversation about better choices. If-then decision-making can work in any number of areas. *If* a student struggles on the second-round district assessment, *then* we will implement Tier 2 interventions. *If* a student is absent more than two days each month, *then* we will contact parents to offer attendance solutions. Think through these scenarios up front, and make your decisions before you need to in the heat of the moment.

The Checklist Mentality

I have used checklists for many years. I think it started when my wife introduced them to me. She has a checklist for everything, and it really helps her to stay organized and accomplish everything on the list. I've also read the productivity experts who say that the small dopamine hit that you get from checking off a mundane task on a checklist is not the way to accomplish meaningful work. Checklists should not be the place where we put our most important work tasks, but they can include the monotonous busywork that defines our days.

The other problem with checklists is that everything on the list has the same importance. Now you can prioritize your checklist (think bento box!) to put your most important tasks at the top of the list or number the items on your checklist to make sure you are hitting the priorities first. David Allen's productivity bible *Getting Things Done* suggests that the importance of a checklist is getting things out of your head and onto a piece of paper or recorded digitally so that they are not stopping you from thinking about other things.

To clarify my love for checklists, part of my system is built around checklists and my notebook. The notebook is a great way to contain all of those unruly checklists that might be found in multiple spots. The notebook helps me to keep my checklists organized. My number one goal in using checklists is to get things out of my head. It is extremely important to write things down. Enter my notebook (and multiple checklists). I use checklists in my notebook for two main reasons (we'll explore more uses of the notebook in the next section):

- Anything that goes into my notebook with a checkbox next to it gets accomplished. It doesn't matter how long it takes me to finish a task; if it is written down in my notebook with a checkbox, it will get done.
- Keeping track of all checklists in one location provides a history of my to-do lists. Everything is in one place. If I need to reference something several months after I accomplished it, I can.

The Notebook

In this section, I'm going to share the significance of the notebook. You may immediately think of Ryan Gosling and Rachel McAdams and the love that they shared. While this is important, I'm not talking about the movie of the same name, but rather the notebook that sits on my desk every day. Each school year, I begin a new notebook. My personal favorite is a Moleskine Classic hardcover with graph paper (easier for checkboxes!). I write the school-year number on the cover and I start the notebook sometime in August, just before the school year begins. The notebook is my lifeline. It helps to keep me organized, helps to document all of my meetings and phone calls, and helps keep all of those pesky sticky notes in one specific location.

Here are some of the different ways that I use the notebook:

A checklist of important tasks that need to be completed. I meticulously record all essential tasks. This serves two key functions. First, my notebook acts as an external memory; once a task is written and checked, I can trust it won't be forgotten. Previously, relying solely on my memory led to overlooking certain details. While some checklist items might not be my top priorities, they hold significance for someone else. Second, this system ensures I consistently follow through on commitments. Regardless of my personal prioritization, a task recorded days ago remains crucial to someone else. I strive to build trust with all stakeholders—teachers, students, and parents—by honoring my word. My notebook guarantees nothing slips through the cracks; if it's documented, it gets done.

Supplementary checklists that need documenting. Throughout the year, I conduct sixty to seventy-five teacher observations, typically spread across three rounds. For each round, I print and tape a checklist into my notebook labeled "Round 1 (or 2 or 3) Observations." This notebook is crucial for ensuring I complete every step of the observation cycle: preconference, classroom observation, formal write-up, and postconference. I use similar checklists within the notebook to track teacher professional development plans, student growth objectives, and other crucial deadlines. Honestly, if I ever lost this notebook—and thankfully, I haven't—I'd be in trouble! It's truly my comprehensive guide, handbook, and essential record of everything I've done, need to do, and plan to do throughout the entire school year.

An important place for meeting notes. While some prefer digital meeting notes, I'm a firm believer in handwritten records. I find it helps me absorb information better, stay engaged, and keeps everything consolidated for easy reference. Need to recall that PD plan deadline? A quick flip through my notes from last week's meeting, and I've got it. Writing things down also helps me pinpoint action items during meetings. Let's be honest, a lot of meeting content could just be an email. But, while I'm taking notes, I mark action items with a checkbox, a simple square, for later attention. Plus, having past notebooks is invaluable. I can easily look back and see when things were handled in previous years.

Discipline notes and parent phone call log. Let's be real, parent phone calls about student discipline aren't exactly a highlight of our days. Early on, I tried separate notebooks and even digital spreadsheets to track these communications. But now, it all lives in one notebook. When I'm working through a conflict with a student, I jot down the basics on a sticky note. That sticky then goes right into the notebook, with a checkbox as a reminder to call home. After I've spoken with the family, I record the details: who I talked to, when, and the outcome. Any resulting action items get their own checkbox. For example, if a parent expresses concern about ongoing conflicts and wants their child separated from another student next year, I'll note that with a checkbox so I remember to adjust the class lists. It's all about keeping it organized and making sure nothing slips through the cracks.

Ideas and brainstorming. I'd like to believe that I have some brilliant ideas, and I'd really like to think I capture them all instantly—but when I don't, poof, they vanish. Picture this: I'm observing a math lesson, and a teacher's approach sparks a great idea for boosting word-problem skills in the upper grades. I'll scribble it down on a sticky note right then and there, and then make absolutely sure it gets transferred to my notebook. Keeping all my ideas, whether they're simple or a bit out-there, means I'll eventually do something with them. It might take months until something else clicks and it's an aha moment: "Wait, this fits perfectly with that idea I had back in the fall. Let me dig that note out."

Anything else that's super important. Whenever I start working with a new consultant, their contact info—name, number, email—goes straight into my notebook. Any crucial details that might come up later have to go in there. During district team meetings, when we're reviewing intervention data, I might use a highlighter to put a big star next to key points I want to share. Important dates, calendar reminders, deadlines, field trip contacts—basically, anything I might need to know lands in the notebook. It's my central hub for all of my essential information.

The notebook is my lifeline. It keeps all parts of my role organized, helps me to ensure that tasks are completed and not forgotten, and keeps information all in one place to be easily found whenever I need it. It also helps to be able to find information when computer systems shut down or don't work.

> **SYSTEMS CHECK**
>
> How do you organize yourself? Are you a good old pen and paper person, or do you keep a digital file of everything? Do you use a hard-copy planner or maintain an online calendar of events?
>
> List any different systems or methods that you use for organization/productivity purposes. Think clearly about how you might consolidate some of these systems or methods into one specific system.

The URGENT Umbrella

A few years ago, we modified our car loop to accommodate more cars and eliminate a backup of traffic on the main road in front of our school. We wanted to ease traffic congestion by moving it from the staff lot to the back blacktop. While this increased capacity, it required more staff and created a clash of urgencies: our staff's priority was student safety, parents wanted to quickly come and go, and kids just wanted to show us all of the cool stuff in their cars. Ultimately, the headaches, including many rain-soaked mornings, led us to eliminate the car loop altogether. We can often get soaked trying to take care of all of the urgent needs of all of our stakeholders. Let me introduce you to the idea of the URGENT umbrella.

We're constantly bombarded with urgent requests from staff, students, parents, and supervisors, all with their own pressing needs. A teacher needs immediate discipline action, a parent is frantic about safety, a student is in pain, and your boss wants an instant budget update. It's a deluge. What you need is an umbrella. The URGENT umbrella is a six-pronged strategy for protecting you from the urgent demands of others that may not be so urgent. You can use the URGENT umbrella to keep you from getting soaked from the demands of all involved. Let's examine the six protective panels of your URGENT umbrella.

When faced with a demand, you need to determine whether it's URGENT:

- Urgency: Is this task something that can wait? Are you going to lose anything by waiting on this task?
- Relevancy: Is this task relevant to what you are working toward? Is it important enough to drop everything else you are working on?
- Gravity: What happens if you don't drop everything to address this? What impact will not doing something have?
- Effort: How much effort will go into completing the task? What type of time and resources will you need to put toward this task?
- Necessity: Is this task absolutely necessary in order to be able to run the school or district? Is it a must?
- Timeline: What is the deadline for this task? How does it fit in with your existing schedule?

Let's quickly run a task under the URGENT umbrella to determine if it's something we need to add to our to-do list. Let's take the example of a parent calling to share their concerns about the lack of a crossing guard in the morning.

Urgency: There are very few students who walk across the crosswalks that this parent is concerned about, and all of those children are accompanied by an adult.

Relevancy: This has not been a concern for anyone else for the past several years, and impacts very few people.

Gravity: If I don't call back this parent to address their concerns, they may call over to the superintendent's office to share the concern.

Effort: If I reach out to the parent via a phone call, I may be on the phone for five to ten minutes. I can also send an email response, which might take a few minutes to craft.

Necessity: This is not a necessity, as the school has been running safely without any issues previously.

Timeline: Ultimately, I don't have control over whether a crossing guard can be hired for the corner the parent is concerned about. I can respond with an email to the parent by the end of the day.

After quickly going through the URGENT Umbrella, I've decided to simply send the parent an email response to let them know that I don't have control over hiring crossing guards, that it is a function of the township police department, but that I will share the concern with our safety coordinator. I'll add a checkbox to my notebook to send this email prior to the end of the school day.

The URGENT umbrella can help you decide which of other people's wants and needs you have to take on yourself. It can protect you from the elements and give you a shield against those that may not be urgent.

Funnel Forward

I remember being at the beach as a kid with my pile of plastic beach toys. There was a shovel, a water wheel, a funnel, and several castle molds. I would shovel in thousands of grains of sand into the funnel and bring it to a smooth, sharp flow going into the castle molds. The funnel allowed for everything all at once to go in, and only a little bit to come out. Using the funnel was soothing. Lots in. A little out. Oh, to have that feeling again!

There will be days when you look at your list of to-do items and feel completely overwhelmed. Know that it will all get done. In order to get over that overwhelming feeling, you need a strategy that helps you whittle down to the basics.

Let's go back to our funnel. How can you get a lot to go in, but have only a little come out? *Funnel forward* is a method that will allow us to streamline, prioritize, and allocate resources. We want to simplify and optimize our administrative tasks. We want to ensure that the most critical tasks are done first. We want our resources to go toward our most important tasks as well. We want to make sure that we set clear, achievable goals, and use our time wisely.

Funnel forward is a way to plan ahead. At the end of the day, you glance at your notebook, and you see that you still have multiple items from the day that you did not finish. In order to funnel forward to the next day, you are going to count down: three, two, one.

Three. Look at your list of items that aren't completed, and pick three that are the major items for tomorrow. If you didn't finish things today, there may be a handful of must-do items that are now for the next day. Identify those three items to tackle as you plan your following day.

Two. Now that you have three items to tackle, you are going to dedicate two resources to these three items. Maybe you'll dedicate an early-morning sixty-minute time block to your items as well as an additional forty-five minute block in the afternoon. Maybe you'll partner with someone during your hour-long block in the morning. Pick your two resources, be they time blocks, collaborators, or delegates, that will help you to accomplish your goals.

One. Finally, you are going to identify the one task that will be your must-do to accomplish as soon as possible the next day. You'll dedicate an early time block and other resources to accomplishing this goal immediately upon arriving at work the next day.

Let's look at an example. Here's my to-do list at the end of a busy but productive Wednesday:

- complete formal observation writeup for second-grade teacher
- plan twenty-minute pop-up PD technology session for Friday
- contact parents to discuss student academic struggles
- review second-round data from district standardized assessments
- write parent letter about upcoming family event in two weeks
- communicate with teachers regarding end-of-day discipline issue

This looks like a big list to start the following day with. We need to streamline, prioritize, and allocate resources to address this long list.

Three. Let's start by narrowing down our list to a manageable three tasks:

- complete formal observation writeup for second-grade teacher
- plan twenty-minute pop-up PD technology session for Friday
- communicate with teachers regarding end-of-day discipline issue

Just from a time-management standpoint, I want to tackle these three items because they are the most time-dependent tasks. I don't want to leave teachers hanging regarding what happened with their students during physical education class at the end of the day. I need to finalize plans for the Friday pop-up PD session, and I need to finish up the written report of the teacher observation that I completed earlier this afternoon. These are the most timely items.

Two. Now I'm going to dedicate two resources to these three tasks. These three items should take about forty-five minutes to complete. Just to be safe, I'll block off sixty minutes in the morning to manage these three items. In addition to the time block, I'll ask our instructional coach to join me from 10:30 a.m. to 11:00 a.m. to help finalize the plan for the pop-up PD. With these two resources decided, I can hopefully tackle all three items.

One. Finally, I'll decide on the one item that must happen first thing in the morning. Prior to students starting at 8:35 a.m., I'll gather the two fifth-grade teachers to share an update on the discipline issue from PE class. Fifteen minutes should be plenty of time to discuss what happened, what consequences were put in place for students, and how we should move forward. With this one item accomplished first thing, I'll be able to dedicate the hour-long block to the other two important items.

Now that you've made a commitment to getting your most important task done and dedicating two resources to other critical tasks, you can go into the next day with a specific plan to address your most pressing needs. Funnel forward. It's as simple as three, two, one.

How to Organize Folders

When I moved into my current role as a building principal, the previous person in the role shared a folder of digital resources with me, including all of her documents. She was retiring and glad to hand everything over to me. In addition, there were several filing cabinets in the main office, featuring folders that housed what I imagine is everything ever produced in the school. The folders included some of the following labels:

- American Education Week
- Bus evacuations
- Equipment repair forms
- Faculty meetings 2012–2013 (I'm not quite sure what happened to any of the other years; also, I started in 2018)
- Laminator (which seemed like it included way too much information)
- Work-related injuries (which was also a little too full for my liking)

Remember, this is only a sample of the folders housed in the filing cabinets. As an experienced administrator new to the building, I knew that I needed a better system for organizing forms and documents than hard-copy folders housed in several large filing cabinets. I decided to organize digitally. The beauty in keeping track of everything digitally is that you can easily re-create, edit, or reuse documents from year to year.

Of course, you probably have your own organization system, which either works really well or doesn't. I'll share a sampling of how I organize my digital folders, demonstrating why taking time to organize in a specific way up front will actually save you more time on the back end.

Rather than keep everything in files that range across a wide variety of topics, events, and forms, I prefer to keep track of files by year. Within each of these folders, I house all of the materials I need that correspond to the year. For example, there are back-to-school resources within each folder. A welcome-back letter to students and families doesn't change much from year to year other than dates. I will copy the document from the previous year's folder, change the dates, and prepare the letter to be distributed to families. Same goes for staff welcome-back letters, opening-week schedules, and anything else back-to-school related.

As the year progresses, other common letters/documents/information that stays the same from year to year gets updated and distributed. Examples include our annual letter about our Halloween parade, staff PD schedules, state testing documents and updates, and facilities checklists. The amount of paperwork that remains the same from year to year is unbelievable. Keeping track of everything by year can make for very easy organization of all of your stuff. It's easy to find, edit, and share with everyone who needs to know.

> **CONTROL PANEL CHECK: A FAMILY FOLDER**
>
> There are many standard forms and documents that families need on a regular basis. I have three school-aged children of my own. I've been caught frantically searching for a document that my kid just told me about that is suddenly due in eleven hours. We've all been there. It's this pain point for me as a parent that led me to creating a Family Folder for our school parents. I send it out at the beginning of the school year and include all relevant documents, forms, schedules, and any other important stuff that families might need at any given point. As the year goes on, we add other important stuff to the folder. It's a one-stop shop for everything that a family might need.
>
> Get your Family Folder up and running today to keep your families up and running tomorrow.

Plug and Play—Why Scripts Are the Solution You Didn't Know You Needed

We've discussed utilizing email templates to make your life easier. Other templates are a great way to become more efficient. Let me share an example.

Each year, we host a moving-up ceremony for our fifth-grade students as they prepare to move on to middle school. When I first became principal in the building, I relied on one of our veteran fifth-grade teachers to share how the ceremony had been conducted in the past. I spent a lot of time preparing all of the names for awards, certificates, and other honors. In addition, I took copious notes during our rehearsals to ensure that everything would go off without a hitch. During the first ceremony, I noticed that each person involved—me, our school counselor, and each of the fifth-grade teachers—had their own notes that would clog up the podium at the front of the auditorium. Sifting through all of the notes was confusing. Speeches would change from year to year, but, for the most part, the ceremony has retained a similar structure and format throughout my time at the school.

A few years in, I wanted to streamline the process because I felt like I was duplicating work each year. I started with a letter that I write to the fifth-grade students that goes in our yearbook. Because I share similar themes with the students each year, I set up a template for my letter. I utilize this same letter as my closing message at our ceremony in June. I also spent considerable time creating a script for the entire ceremony. The script features exactly what each person will say and when it will occur. The script runs several pages and also includes all of the awards presentations that happen the same way every year.

What's great about the script is that it is now completely plug and play. Each year, I create a copy of the script and just update the names for awards. Most of the new information that needs to be updated can be found in our program, so the updating of the script is something that can easily be delegated to multiple people involved in the awards ceremony. Mostly everything else about the script, except for the students, stays the same from year to year. The other beautiful thing about the script is that it keeps us to a specified time. I can put the ceremony on the calendar from 9:30 a.m. to 10:15 a.m. and know that we will be done in anywhere from forty to forty-five minutes every year.

There are probably multiple events that you do each year that could benefit from a script, including graduation ceremonies, Back to School Night events, assemblies, awards ceremonies, musical and theatrical performances, Career Day, and more.

> **SYSTEMS CHECK**
>
> What annual events do you hold that would benefit from a script?
>
> Pick one of those events, and begin a script. It may take you a little bit of time up front, but, trust me, you will appreciate this step next year, when all you have to do is plug and play!

Preflight Checklist for Streamlining Your Workflows

- ❏ What strategy would you like to try?
- ❏ Why? (your true north)
- ❏ How? (your plan)
- ❏ When? (your timeline)

CREATING A FOCUSED, PRODUCTIVE ENVIRONMENT

Steve Jobs famously said, "People think focus means saying yes to the thing you've got to focus on. But that's not what it means at all. It means saying no to the hundred other good ideas that there are. You have to pick carefully."

He couldn't be more right. Cultivating a focused and productive environment is a necessity. In this chapter, we will create a to-don't list, build a culture of productivity, celebrate our wins, organize our work area, and develop focused time to get stuff done.

Avoid Your To-Do List. Try a To-Don't List Instead.

I've already written about the importance of my notebook and the checklists that I maintain there to keep myself completely organized. The to-do list can be a savior to those trying to be productive and systematic, but the opposite type of list might be helpful as well. Maybe what you need is to completely avoid the to-do list altogether. If you are hyperfocused on getting everything checked off your list but can't because too many other distractions are getting in the way, maybe you need a to-don't list.

The idea of a to-don't list comes from Tania Katan in her book, *Creative Trespassing*. Tania suggests that you "make a list of all of the crap you do to avoid your dreams. Be honest and detailed." The idea is to write down everything that holds us back from getting to the things that we actually want to work on. In our schools, there are many time-consuming tasks that take up our days and keep us from our important work. Instead of adding one more of those items to our to-do list, let's list all of the things that are holding us back.

When I first read Tania's book over the summer a few years ago, I decided to generate my own list prior to the start of a new school year. My to-don't list looked like this:

Don't:

- spend more time in the office, at my desk, answering emails, or completing administrative tasks
- instantly judge a student or assume that I know exactly what the problem is and how I can "fix" it
- respond without listening and understanding first
- read from bulleted slides during staff meetings
- dedicate my energy to too many projects, initiatives, and tasks—without focus
- stick to traditions simply for the sake of sticking to traditions
- complain about a problem without proposing a solution
- assume that I know better because of my position or title
- force students to adhere to rules or expectations simply for the sake of compliance
- use data to make a decision without considering the whole story behind the data

When you think critically about the things that you should not be doing, it can help to provide clarity about what you should be doing. When you start to slip back into your bad habits, the to-don't list can help to recenter you and provide direction for what you are actually trying to accomplish. For me the list is a reminder of all of the things that stop me from being my most productive. The list also helps me to focus on what matters most.

So, take a moment, and outline your own to-don't list. While we've shared a great deal about productivity and your accomplishments so far in the book, use this opportunity to focus on what you don't want to accomplish.

Creating a Culture of School Productivity

When you go on autopilot, you are going to inspire others around you to become more productive. You'll find that others inquire about your methods. You'll find teachers who are interested in learning more about how you are minimizing and streamlining your work. When you begin to model specific ways of doing things, like not sending emails outside of school hours, honoring colleagues' personal lives, and finding time for the important parts of your day, others will start to embrace the mindset. Productivity will become contagious.

Try the following strategies for creating a culture of productivity within your school or district.

Host a priority PD session instead of a staff meeting. Have you ever canceled a staff meeting and given the unexpected free time back to colleagues? Were you viewed as a hero by your staff? I love sending an email canceling a meeting and giving staff the time to do some necessary work. Instead of your monthly meeting, host a priority PD where you give time for everyone to meet to focus on meaningful priorities. Staff can work individually to focus on necessary items, or the priority PD session can be hosted in a common space where staff can collaborate to work more efficiently. Give everyone time back to focus on priorities. It's well worth it.

Provide professional development. Model your methods. At a staff meeting, share one of your productivity strategies with staff. Host an autopilots assembly in which you and colleagues gather together and share different ideas for productivity. How do you tackle your email? Can you share your methods with colleagues and learn more about how they tackle their paperwork responsibilities? Highlight a staff productivity tip in your weekly newsletter or at a monthly meeting. Connecting and sharing your best ways to be more efficient is going to move your culture of productivity forward.

Teach students productivity principles. Autopilot strategies are not only going to help teaching and administrative staff; the methods and strategies can also help students as well. Showing and modeling organization, productivity, and time management will help students as they progress into the workforce or higher education. Likewise, students will be able to share their time-management hacks and shortcuts. We can learn just as much from them as they can from us.

Take things off plates. If you can eliminate needless busywork for colleagues, they will absolutely buy into the culture of productivity you are promoting. Many of the things that we add to teachers' plates are needless busywork, things that can instead be automated or streamlined to make everyone's lives easier. Each year, the state requires teachers to create a professional development plan (PDP) that documents their required professional development hours. It's very bureaucratic and time-consuming for no real reason. Instead of making teachers create their own PDP, I create one that applies to all teachers in the building, supplying them with a template including the already-written goals. All teachers need to do is cut and paste into a formal PDP document. Show teachers how to be more productive, and start by giving them more of their time back.

Promote well-being. Let colleagues know that it's OK to focus on well-being. Make sure you are honoring staff's lives outside of school.

Don't ask for unnecessary tasks to be completed when they can be eliminated instead. Help staff members to focus on productivity in order to improve their lives, not just to add more stuff. One of the reasons you want to take things off the plate is to avoid burnout. When we ask teachers why they are struggling in their jobs, one of the answers I consistently hear is that the extra stuff like administrative tasks is too much when added on to trying to work with students. Being more efficient means taking time for yourself as well. Promote this with staff.

Honor no-meeting weeks. Scheduling time to meet with teachers can be incredibly difficult. At Yardville, teachers have a daily forty-minute prep time where they can meet with their grade-level partner. It's also one of the daily times that I can meet with teachers. Several of our regular routines, like grade-level meetings and data meetings, occur during teacher prep periods. It can be frustrating for teachers who have other priorities to have their precious time taken away. Try to recognize a no-meeting week, during which you stick to not taking any of this valuable time away. It will be appreciated and provide time for more productive and meaningful work.

Create a Distraction List

You are working on next year's class schedule in your office and you've done everything you can to avoid distraction. You've put up the Do Not Disturb sign on your door. You've put your phone away and asked your assistants to hold all calls. You have all of your previous schedules lying on your desk, and you're ready to get to work.

But first, you check your email and get distracted by a message from a parent. You quickly type a response and turn your attention back to the schedule. You decide to start with the lunch schedules.

As you think about what the lunch schedules look like, you stop to check the weather online for afternoon dismissal.

You get right back to it and attempt to actually create some schedules. Another thought pops into your mind. You forgot to tell your family that you would be late tonight because you have to stay for a PTA meeting. You quickly find your phone to send a quick text. So far, you've been working for about fifteen minutes of the half hour you blocked off. And you haven't gotten much done. In fact, zero schedules have been created.

It doesn't matter what you are attempting to accomplish and how much you try to limit distractions. Inevitably, things will pop up, thoughts will run through your mind, distractions will try to get you. When those thoughts arise, the worst thing is to stop what you're doing to address them. I'm going to propose a different strategy.

In your notebook, add a page for a distraction list. Start a blank page, and write "Distractions" at the top. Whenever you are working on something important, and suddenly get pulled away by a thought, jot down the idea on the distractions page. That email from a parent? Jot it down. That text you need to send to your family? Jot down a note. Checking the weather? Jot it down.

After you've actually created schedules because you haven't let the distractions take over, you can get back to your distraction list. It's OK to have those distracting thoughts. It's not OK to let them take over. Just jot them down. Forget them, and go back to what you should be doing. The thoughts are out of your mind, on your distraction list, and you can get back to them as soon as you're done focusing. Leave your distractions to the distraction list. Get busy instead.

Parade Through the Rain

Our school hosts an annual Halloween parade that is attended by hundreds of parents, grandparents, and other family members. It is one of the highlights of the early school year, and it draws an enthusiastic crowd. Every year, I fret as I monitor the weather forecast leading up to the day of the parade. Our backup plan for the parade is always to host the parade indoors, sans all of the family members and fanfare. On a few occasions, we have had to go to this backup plan.

It's always a very painful decision to make because it ends up disappointing a lot of people who want to witness the pageantry of the day. But rather than choose a rain date, we have paraded through slight rain drops and paraded indoors despite the rain drops. Your autopilot plan has to work in a similar manner. You've got to move forward no matter what. Parade through the rain when you need to. Have a backup to your backup for when things don't go according to plan. Being productive means being able to adjust and shift to something else when things don't go exactly as planned.

Let's think about a specific example. Let's imagine that you are sitting in the second of four scheduled observations on your calendar for the day. Midway through the observation, your computer starts to lose power. You don't have a charger. You could run down and grab it from your office, but you'd miss the most important part of the lesson. This is where you need to be prepared to parade through the rain. As the computer goes completely dead, you pull out your phone and begin to snap pictures of what the students are working on so that you can finish up the observation once your computer is safely on your charging dock in the confines of your office.

There is no rest for the weary, though, as your next observation begins in three minutes. You quickly run back to your office, throw the computer on its charging dock, and grab the greatest observation tools ever invented: a yellow legal pad and a pen. You write up the observation on paper, take a picture of the notes, and upload them into your observation recording tool before assigning scores for the observation. Despite your computer deciding that today was not the day for four observations, you still managed to be productive and get all of them done.

We will refer to this as the parade-through-the-rain rule. When life throws you rain, or sleet, or hail, don't stop what you're doing. Parade through it no matter what. Be productive even if everyone and everything around you are not cooperating. Have a backup to your backup plan. No one said that going on autopilot meant that you would always see sunny skies. When the rain clouds appear on the horizon, have your poncho ready, figure out what you'll do next, and don't waste any time on the decision to move forward.

Celebrate Productivity Wins

You will go home at the end of the day, and you will have one of two feelings. Sometimes, you'll feel like you won. Other times, you won't. This next part is about those days when you feel like you won.

Buy a gong. What could be cooler than having a large (or even small) gong in your school to celebrate a project finish? Place the gong in a well-used space, and whenever you are able to accomplish one of your goals, walk out to it and give it a good bang! Encourage others to use the got-it-done gong whenever they finish a task or project. Soon, you'll create a culture of productivity wins.

Celebrate with an accountability partner. You are more likely to reach your goals when you announce them to someone else who will hold you accountable. Pick an accountability partner, and share your projects and goals with them. Likewise, they can share their goals with you, which makes both of you more likely to be productive and finish your tasks. Once completed, you and your accountability partner can host a small celebration by going out after school for a cup of coffee, providing a bag of candy as a reward, or just exchanging fun cards to recognize your wins.

Recognize a pro pro of the week. Send out a quick email at the end of the week celebrating a pro(ductivity) pro(fessional) of the week. Recognize someone for the wonderful way that they conducted a data analysis, or how efficient they were in completing a project with students. Sharing some love for the pro pro and highlighting a different productivity win each week will further strengthen the culture of productivity in your school or district.

Productivity tools as gifts. I may be a pen snob, but there is nothing like the feeling of discovering a brand-new pen that writes really well. I have settled on my pen of choice—the Sharpie S-Gel pen—and I can't tell you how excited others are when they are able to "steal" one from my office. Recognize others for their productivity wins by giving them productivity tools. Give out unique pens and sticky notes. Order some quality pens with your school logo on it, or pens in fun colors. Give away uniquely shaped sticky notes; stars and hearts are a lot of fun. Recognize fellow productivity gurus with tools to help them capture the fun and adventure of back-to-school shopping, discovering all of those new tools and gadgets that can inspire them to be more efficient.

Start a done streak. Comedian Jerry Seinfeld has talked about his strategy for comedy writing. While explaining how difficult it can be to sit down each day and write down comedy bits, he shared a rather simple way to celebrate his prolific writing. Each day that he was able to sit down and write jokes, he would mark that date on a desk calendar with a big X. If he did it two days in a row, he would have two X's—a done streak. His goal, once he got going, was not to break his streak of joke writing. Start your own streak of completing your daily goals. How many days in a row can you go? I used to use this strategy to keep track of a daily writing streak. I used a specific app called Done to track my progress, which started to get a little wonky after I wrote each day for approximately 725 straight days. Start your done streak today!

Airplane Mode and Cave Time

We have a saying in education that many administrators often wield to show how committed they are to communicating with colleagues: "My door is always open."

I've been on interview panels for other administrative positions where it feels as if every candidate has uttered these five words when asked about their management style. The problem with this statement is the lack of truth in it. If your door is always open, then someone will come in to talk to you about some personal matter, and you will actually have to close the door for some privacy. I guess "My door is open most of the time until I have to close it" isn't quite as catchy.

There are times when we need to close our doors and not be bothered. I know that this may be a hot take, but sometimes it's actually nice to work interruption free. As a school leader, it is very hard to have any moments of downtime to accomplish something meaningful. If you abide by the door-is-always-open policy, then, even when the door is closed, others will think nothing of opening to interrupt for "just one second." I lived by the door-is-always-open rule at one point, and I can clearly say that no one thought anything of knocking or interrupting when the door was closed.

Another part of this problem is our constant connection to the outside world via our phones. Even if you are huddled snugly in your office with the door closed and a note with poster-sized letters that say, "DON'T BOTHER ME!" people can still reach out to you via your phone. I have always given staff members my cell phone number in case they need to reach me in any situation. Throughout the day, I often receive text messages from colleagues no matter where I am in the building, even if that is behind closed doors. And if staff members don't interrupt, family members and friends certainly will. The Czyz family's text chain often blows up several times a day with reminders, schedule updates, and general well wishes that sometimes come at very inopportune times.

As I said, it can be very hard to close the door and have a period of uninterrupted time. I'm going to propose two solutions here that have sometimes worked for me.

Airplane mode. We all know it exists (at least I hope everyone has at least heard of it). You can put your phone in airplane mode, which will limit your access to the internet, calling and text features, and other apps on your phone. When I am trying to not be interrupted, I will utilize airplane mode to give myself a period of quiet to accomplish whatever important task I am working on. One of the tasks that I generally use airplane mode for is when I am writing something, such as a letter to parents or a presentation I am preparing for a board meeting. Airplane mode allows me to have a sense of quiet, whereas leaving the phone in its normal state means that people might interrupt my state of flow. It's much easier to write when I can focus unfettered by any distractions.

Cave time. Let me suggest another strategy that might also be helpful. We can both agree that it is OK to close the door sometimes. I'm going to go as polar opposite to the rule as I can and suggest that, instead of leaving the door open, you not only close it, but barricade it, turn off the lights, and pretend no one is even in there. You will be in there, cut off from the rest of the world, gloriously finishing some of your most important work. I refer to this as *cave time*.

During cave time, I will close my door, and turn off the lights. The lights are a key factor, because if people even catch a glimpse of the possibility of you being in your office, they will knock and share whatever burden they currently have. While sitting in my office with the lights down low, I have heard would-be interrupters ask the secretaries, "Is he in there?" Not wanting to lie, I've heard and respected their response of "I'm not sure." People normally go away at this point if the lights are off. No one ever expects you to sit in the dark. Cave time can be used when you are frantically trying to beat a deadline, or when an emergency situation presents itself, and undisturbed time is of the essence.

The Importance of the Office

Now you may read the title of this section and know that I'm immediately going to talk about what geniuses the writers of *The Office* were. Those scripts were simply magic. They perfectly captured how daily, mundane things could be interesting at the Scranton branch of Dunder Mifflin, and the actors brought to life something that will live forever as a classic TV comedy.

In fact, though, I'm not talking about the TV show. Rather, I'm referring to the place where your desk is housed and where you get a lot of your important work done. Our offices serve as our homes away from home. What our offices look like can tell us a lot about the people who work in them.

You've read a considerable part of the book at this point. If you had to guess, what do you think my office space is like? Considering that I'm a huge fan of efficiency and productivity, you might guess that my office is pretty organized and clutter free. If you were thinking of my office somewhere around 8:00 a.m. or 4:30 p.m., you'd be right. But during the day, you might find papers strewn across the table, sticky notes littering my desktop, multiple screens featuring open documents and tabs, and more than five pens tossed into every corner of my workspace. The pens are ready and waiting for someone to walk into my office and ask me to sign something. I always want to be ready for efficiency, and maybe, deep down, I have a fear of not being able to find a quality pen at that exact moment.

I am very particular about the way my office is set up. On the day I started at my new school, I called the custodian to the office and asked him to remove the monstrosity of a three-sided desk that took up half of the space. I replaced it with a small round table at which I could hold conversations with people. I also kept a small desk and ordered an additional element that allows me to convert it to a standing desk. Eighty to ninety percent of the day, the desk is in standing mode, as I'm constantly coming and going. While my office is not big by any stretch of the imagination, I have managed to create several distinctive zones for my work:

- My computer screens sit atop the standing desk and connect to my laptop. This is the digital home for getting stuff done.
- A four-by-eight-foot whiteboard along the back wall serves as my collaboration and brainstorming space.
- Opposite the whiteboard is a dry-erase board, four-month calendar, which I update at the end of each month to add the

next one. This is my go-to when I'm quickly trying to find a date, even more so than my digital calendar.
- A small round table hosts meetings with students, staff, and parents, and sometimes holds a mess of papers as I'm trying to organize several things at once.
- Finally, I have a small butcher-block table recycled from the kitchen that sits in the corner of the office to serve as a place to sit and write a quick letter or complete some more serious work.

My office works for me. It's taken me a long time to get to the point of having these distinctive zones, but, despite the size of my office, I feel like I'm able to focus on specific things in each area. In addition, my notebook and several hundred sticky notes are constantly available, always ready to add something important to my process.

Your office is one of the most important things to consider in trying to go the autopilot route. Think of your office as the place where your most important work gets done, and any kind of poor planning or inefficiency can cause dangerous problems.

You need to think critically about how you design and use your office space. Without a careful plan, you may waste time, opportunity, and effort in how you do things. An office should be designed for efficiency and flow, not slow you down in accomplishing all of your goals. Consider the following questions when looking at your office space and deciding if you are using the space in a productive manner suitable for autopilot purposes:

- What type of work are you trying to get done in your office?
- Do you have a separate meeting space, or will meetings be happening in your office?
- What lighting source are you using? Is there enough natural light?
- How can you optimally set up furniture to ensure workflow?

- Do you have comfortable seating? Will you be able to sit for extended periods of time?
- Is the space welcoming to parents, students, and staff?
- Do you have flexibility in the office design to accommodate updates or expansions within the space?

Having worked in several different school districts, I've had a number of different offices during my time as an administrator. Some were better (more spacious and better views) than others. Some provided me with more flexibility, and others limited where I could put technology depending on where the connections were. I've shared office space several times with others, which makes you think critically about your part of the space and how you function in it. I can honestly say that I've learned something from each space that I've worked in as an administrator.

If you are in your first office as a school administrator, and you were focused on a million other things when you started the job, you may not have given your space much thought. I'm encouraging you to spend some time thinking about your office now. You need to be able to create a space that works for you, allows for efficiency and productivity, and gives you an overall sense of joy about where you are working. It could be that the furniture you inherited from the previous administrator doesn't fit your style or work particularly well. Your comfort will ultimately aid your productivity. Spend time thinking about how you want to use your office, and dedicate time to designing it in that way.

The office is the place where you spend the majority of your time at work. Make it your happy place. Don't let a lack of thinking about it cause you one more moment of inefficiency. Start now by completing the next systems check.

> **SYSTEMS CHECK**
>
> - What does your office space look like?
> - Have you considered the design and flow of your office?
> - Do you have easy access to the things you need?
> - Do you need to declutter?
> - How can you improve your workspace?

> **CONTROL PANEL CHECK: DESKTOP ORGANIZER**
>
> What is the one thing that you need to order for your office? There is one absolute must that I can't live without. It's a desktop organizer with hard plastic sleeves to organize documents so I can have them at my fingertips when needed. Mine contains all of the documents that I reference on a regular basis without needing to look them up in their digital format:
>
> - school maps and room numbers
> - staff list
> - school and district calendars
> - district phone directory
> - schedules (full day, half day, and delayed opening)
> - observation and walk-through rounds
> - class lists
> - staff birthdays
>
> You don't actually know how many times you reference any of these papers until you're looking for one and can't find it in the cloud. I'm not going to recommend that you purchase a bunch of productivity stuff—but this one I must. Get yourself a desktop page organizer right now. It will make your life so much easier.

Preflight Checklist for Creating a Focused, Productive Environment

- ❑ What strategy from this chapter would you like to try?
- ❑ Why? (your true north)
- ❑ How? (your plan)
- ❑ When? (your timeline)

ROUTINES AND RITUALS FOR SUCCESS

As Aristotle wisely noted, "We are what we repeatedly do. Excellence, then, is not an act, but a habit."

Let's explore how building intentional routines and rituals can transform those habits into a solid foundation for our continued successes. In this chapter, we will build routines to limit distractions, create shutdown rituals, overcome Sunday nights, and discover the best time to plan.

No-Office Days and No-Distraction Days

We've explored a lot of strategies for dealing with the administrative tasks and minutiae that often fill our day. The majority of our work as school leaders involves striking a balance between the administrative busywork and work with students and teachers. One way that going on autopilot helps us is by giving us time back to get into classrooms to visit with teachers and students.

Two strategies that I want to share in this section serve as opposite markers of our commitment to both the administrative part of our jobs and the people-person part of our jobs. We know that we can't do one without the other, and, if we commit more time to one over the other, the imbalance causes us to struggle in our positions.

The first strategy is regularly implementing no-office days. This is a day just like it sounds. You are barred from the office for the bulk of the day. The idea is to get you out among the people (students and staff). You can visit classrooms and converse with colleagues while also seeing what students are doing in the classroom. On days when you are stuck in your office, bound to a two-hour virtual meeting, it can be nice to get out and about among the people. I used to regularly schedule no-office days and try to adhere to actually staying out of the office. I set up a portable desk (on wheels) in our school hallway to allow me to check or send a quick email even as I was sharing time or space with our classes. The portable desk idea allowed me to commit to the no-office day in a way that I might not have been able to without the space to work.

Even if you can manage to schedule one no-office day a month, it can help serve as a powerful connection point with your staff and students. The key is being able to get out of your office because you have automated or delegated enough of your busywork that you won't be swamped when you get back into your office the next day.

You may want to pair your no-office day once a month with a no-distraction day. This is when you close your door and take care of the administrative tasks and projects that are hounding you and need to be done. If you can get everything on your to-do list done on a no-distraction day, it can give you the time necessary to host a no-office day. Even if you are not able to schedule a full day for no-distraction day, a half day may serve the purpose as well.

Each year, I schedule a no-distraction (half) day prior to our school budget deadline. Leading up to the day, I add all of my budget materials to a folder, send out emails to staff for budgeting feedback and requests, and pull last year's budget. I block out a full two hours on the calendar, close my door, and hunker down. My goal at the end of the two hours is to have my main budget completed, along with tentative budgets that include 5 percent and 10 percent cuts. Using a no-distraction day allows me to go into our district budget meetings fully prepared to answer any questions that central office administrators may have.

Without blocking out specific time, it's hard to dedicate the time required to the annual budget. No-distraction days, however, work like a charm.

Schedule Your Decisions

In a *School Administration* article from June 2018, researchers McDaniel and Gruenert showed that a school administrator can make, on average, from three to five hundred decisions per day. Now, I've never tracked my own decision-making throughout a day, but I would imagine it is somewhere in the hundreds. On a typical day, an administrator might deal with small decisions at any given point (answering a staff question, approving a purchase order, etc.) and larger decisions (handling a disciplinary case, planning a staff professional development session, etc.). Working to make all of these decisions can add to your efficiency conundrum as the decisions pile up throughout the day and take away from other things that you had planned. Often, you need to make decisions in the heat of the moment and move on, despite the outcome of your decision.

Have you ever been faced with a decision as an administrator that you didn't want to make? You put it off. Hemmed and hawed. You waited until the very last minute before the deadline to make the decision. And with all of this worry and stress over the decision, was it any different than if you made a snap judgment quickly at the beginning of the process?

There is certainly something to be said for making informed decisions. You have information about either of your choices and decide based on the best possible outcome. There's also research to say that sometimes our snap decisions are our best initial judgments, and we shouldn't waste a lot of time in the decision-making process.

I want to propose that we dedicate more time to our decision-making process. A lot of my decisions are often forced by the time involved. Suddenly, a project deadline is looming, so I have to address a decision that I've either been dreading or haven't even considered. Let's instead plan to schedule our decisions. Again, many of the decisions that you make throughout the day are going to be snap judgments that you won't have time to schedule. When I say *schedule your decisions*, I want you to provide a focused time dedicated to the decisions that you need to make. Your decision time is part scheduling, part decision-making, and part long-term planning. Set a time at the beginning or end of your week to review, and then plan your upcoming week. You'll look at the decisions that may be looming and come up with a time frame for making your decisions. Let me share an example.

I love utilizing Friday afternoons as my reflection and planning period. I sit in my quiet office, as most people leave right at the last bell to get home for the weekend. With quiet focus, I'm able to review exactly what I accomplished for the week and take a look at my upcoming week. Let's say that I have the following upcoming tasks or projects that need to be completed:

- plan teacher professional development day
    - check with tech facilitator for availability
    - create agenda
    - review slide presentation
- complete classroom walk-throughs for first and second grades
- submit detailed budget to business office
    - 100 percent version
    - 5 percent cut
    - 10 percent cut

- meet with School Improvement Panel to discuss walk-through data

This seems like a full list for the upcoming week, with several tasks that will keep me busy, in addition to all of the fires that may arise. I want to schedule each of these tasks for the upcoming week so that I'm not letting decisions loom over my head all weekend. I know that the teacher PD day is a week from next Tuesday, so I want to make sure that this gets taken care of by Thursday or Friday. I'll schedule an email (for Monday at 8:00 a.m.) to the tech facilitator now, with the hopes of having an answer by Tuesday. I'll complete the agenda for the PD day on Tuesday, and review my slides by Wednesday. Everything should be ready to go by Thursday.

My budget meeting is on Friday, and I want to make sure I have full budget details prepared, along with a 5 percent and 10 percent cut, just in case. I'll start on the budget first thing on Monday morning so that it can be completed and reviewed before my Friday meeting. Thursday looks like the only good morning to meet with the School Improvement Panel, so I'll schedule the meeting for 8:15 a.m. Finally, because I'll want to include the walk-through data from first and second grades at our School Improvement Panel meeting, I'll schedule the classroom walk-throughs on Wednesday, then quickly review the data before Thursday's meeting.

This type of thought process around the planning and scheduling of decisions helps to ensure that, even with all of the other minutiae and fires that you are dealing with, you'll still get your important work done. As I leave on Friday, after I've scheduled my decisions for the following week, my updated list will look like this:

- plan teacher professional development day
- check with tech facilitator for availability—NOW—schedule for Monday @ 8:00 a.m.
- create agenda—Tuesday @ 9:30 a.m.
- review slide presentation—Wednesday @ 9:30 a.m.

- complete classroom walk-throughs for first and second grades—Wednesday @ 10:30 a.m.
- submit detailed budget to business office—Friday—10:30 a.m. meeting
- 100 percent version—Monday @ 9:30 a.m.
- 5 percent cut—Monday @ 9:30 a.m.
- 10 percent cut—Monday @ 9:30 a.m.
- meet with School Improvement Panel to discuss walk-through data—Thursday @ 8:15 a.m.

I can now go into the weekend with no decisions to make about how any of this work will be completed the following week. I shouldn't have any lingering thoughts about what I need to do or how I'm going to do it. Of course, there may be some pressing matters that interrupt something that is scheduled, but by scheduling all of these decisions and leaving white space in the schedule in case emergencies come up, I should be able to tackle each of these projects in a timely and efficient manner. Spend some time scheduling your decisions. It's a helpful step in making sure you reach your autopilot goals.

End-of-Day Shutdown Rituals and Routines

Have you ever frantically rushed out of the office at the end of the day thinking you were done, only to worry, stress, and fret over nine things you still felt hanging over your head? If so, it's normal. This is something that happens to all of us from time to time. But if it's happening frequently, you may need to put a shutdown routine in place to help you leave everything at work and keep your at-home time sacred.

Let's think about what a shutdown routine might look like. I like to come into my office following afternoon dismissal of students and check any last emails that need an immediate response. If emails don't require an immediate response, I may move them to my Today or This Week folder for later action. After I close email for the day, I review my notebook to see if there are any tasks or customer support tickets that I haven't gotten to that can be easily addressed now that I have a few free minutes. I'll also add any goals or tasks that I want to start on the next morning. It's good to have your marching orders as soon as you come in the next day. It allows you to hit the ground running. My other objective for my end-of-day shutdown is to get everything out of my head and into the notebook so that I have nothing to worry about or focus on when I'm at home with other priorities.

I like to use a specific protocol called *reflect, review, to-do* that helps with the end-of-day routine.

Reflect. What went well today? What didn't go so well? What emergencies or fires came up that stopped me from being productive today?

Review. What did I accomplish from my list of meaningful goals today? If you are using the bento box method, did you get your main goals done today?

To-do. Let me write down my goals or tasks that I want to accomplish tomorrow. If I know that they are written down, I don't have to worry about them at all tonight.

Productivity guru Cal Newport suggests building a specific shutdown ritual that helps you mindfully separate your work priorities from your home priorities. My ritual includes a final check and responses to any open emails that can be addressed. I then turn off my computer for the day. Next, I add to the notebook any specific tasks that need to be completed for tomorrow. I close the notebook and place it in a desk drawer to be retrieved in the morning. This specific gesture lets me know that I am done with my work tasks for the day. They have been put away, and tomorrow is another day to get to them. The ritual, along with my thirty-minute drive home, helps me to forget and decompress before I walk in the door at home.

Think about what you can do to implement an end-of-day routine or ritual to help you be more successful and efficient.

> **CONTROL PANEL CHECK: READ LATER**
>
> There are probably a ton of messages that come through your inbox that you may want to read—but not right now. You don't want those things clogging up your inbox taking up valuable space from more meaningful messages. The option is out there to identify those messages and set them in a specific folder to read later. Do you get a number of email newsletters that you enjoy reading, but only when you have the time? You can set them as Read Later and have them delivered to a different inbox for later consumption. The same applies for any number of emails that you probably receive each day but don't need to read right away.
>
> Let's get cracking with Read Later for emails. Save your time for messages that matter first!

The Seven Stages of Sunday Night

Sunday evenings for educators can be extremely difficult. We've all been there before.

As four o'clock on Sunday afternoon rolls around, you start to get that feeling deep inside of you. It starts with shock. You look at your watch, and realize that your weekend has just a few more hours. You try to do anything you can to enjoy the last few hours, but everything you try is filled with a sense of dread and anxiety. You plant yourself in front of the television hoping to take your mind off it. You glance at your watch again.

Six o'clock. Shock quickly turns into denial. You refuse to believe that your weekend is almost over. You think about all of the things you need to do before the morning to be ready for the week, but you momentarily put them off to extend the weekend. You call a friend to chat on the phone, but she quickly hangs up because of some lame excuse about making sure she is ready for the week. You check your watch.

Seven o'clock. Anger takes hold. You are visibly upset as you take out the ironing board to prepare some clothes for the week. Or at least for Monday. You begin the bargaining stage. You decide you'll iron just one outfit, then try to spend thirty minutes reading that book you never got to this weekend. As you sit down to read, you can't focus. You keep looking at your watch.

Now it's 7:34 p.m. . . . 7:52 p.m. . . . 8:09 p.m. Time just seems like it's melting away at this point. You lament everything that you didn't do this weekend and avoid thinking back to any of the joyful moments that you did have. You wonder what you can still accomplish in the last few minutes before you try to go to sleep. Is it already . . .

Eight fifteen. You recognize the feelings of sadness and wonder how this happens to you each and every Sunday night. You wish it wasn't this way, but you can't really do anything about it, can you? You check your bag to make sure you have everything you need for Monday. You return that project folder back to your bag. The reason you brought it home in the first place is that you had every intention of getting to it. You know what they say about the best-laid plans.

Nine o'clock. You decide that you'll shower and get to bed early so that you will at least feel refreshed in the morning. A solid eight hours will do you well. You've accepted it. Monday is almost here. It's coming no matter what. You don't really have control over it anyway.

Nine forty-five. You check your work email to make sure that there are no surprises come morning. It's that one email that you shouldn't have read that keeps your mind going as you lie in bed. You try to think alternate thoughts, but the email is driving you bonkers.

Ten o'clock. 10:12 p.m. . . . 10:48 p.m. . . . 11:03 p.m. . . . 11:57 p.m. You continuously glance at your phone to see what time it is. Each time, you calculate how many hours of sleep you'll get if you just fall asleep this instant. You don't. And you won't. Until sometime after two in the morning. This is simply because exhaustion has taken hold.

We've all been there. We've all sat through the seven stages of Sunday night. For many of us, it happens each week. The anxiety slowly creeps in on Sunday and crowds out every other possible feeling that we can have, especially joy. It's hard to feel joyful—unless, of course, you have Monday off.

How can you bring back that joyful feeling (even if you are not off on Monday)? Try these strategies for making the most of Sundays.

Act like a child. Do you remember what Sundays were like when you were a kid? After Sunday service, I would always race into my room to plan out the remainder of my day. I would somehow manage to cram thirty-seven hours of play/games/projects and plain old fooling around into those remaining eight hours of Sunday. There wasn't a single minute of anxiety that crept into my day. I would always skip directly to the acceptance stage as early as possible on Sunday morning, then jam-pack my day with joy. Why can't we feel this way as adults? Yes, we have a lot more to worry about as adults, but we shouldn't let it ruin a perfectly good Sunday. The worry can wait until Monday morning!

Turn any other time into your Sunday. For many, it's the logistical details and planning for the week that interrupts their Sunday. At best, it starts somewhere late in the evening. At worst, it gobbles up your entire Sunday. I always dread heading to the grocery store on Sundays. I know that if I don't do it, we won't have the food and supplies we need for the week. On many occasions, we have planned activities on Friday night and all day Saturday, so I have no choice but to hit the supermarket on Sunday. Of course, everyone else has the same plan. Create a different routine. Have you ever been to the grocery store on a Friday night around 9:00 p.m.? Try it sometime. It's glorious. You may very well be the only person there. It almost becomes, dare I say it, a joyful experience. Take all of those Sunday routines and weekly prep rituals and move them to a different time. You'll be able to take back your Sundays again.

Disconnect. Tiffany Shlain founded the Webbys, an awards ceremony that honors the best of the internet each year, so it's interesting that she also helped coin the term *Technology Shabbat* in 2010 to describe a day of rest from all screens: phones, computers, tablets, and television. Observing a digital Sabbath can be a great way to increase the time you spend doing something meaningful on a Sunday. Can you imagine not looking at any screen all day? You probably can't. I have a tough time thinking about it as well. But imagine the joy of curling up and reading a good book all day, or taking a hike at a local park with your family. The possibilities are endless.

Sunday Night Write (or whatever it is that you enjoy most!). You may have guessed, but one of the activities that I enjoy most is writing. I will often cap off my weekend by sitting in my writing space and banging away on the keyboard. Yes, I realize that this directly contradicts the previous suggestion of disconnecting, but I'm actively making a choice about how I'm using my computer, and it brings me joy. Take time on Sunday to do whatever it is that you most enjoy. Maybe it's painting. Maybe it's listening to the latest album by one of your favorite musicians. Maybe it's playing music yourself. Maybe you'll be baking a dessert for your family. Include time for the activity that brings you maximum joy and make it a part of your weekly Sunday ritual.

Discover something new. Building in routines will help you to better manage the seven stages, but you should also leave room for things that are new and exciting. Have you ever been rock climbing? Go down and find out what it's all about at your local indoor rock-climbing gym. Find a local museum with a cool new exhibit, and go check it out. Visit a vintage clothing store and pick up some old-but-new threads. Again, the possibilities are endless. Mix in something fresh and novel to bring a sense of joy and excitement to your Sunday.

See Sunday for what it is. At the end of the day, Sunday is just another day, twenty-four hours long like any other day during the week. Treat it that way. Shift your mindset to recognize that each day holds equal importance. Give Sunday its rightful due as another day to experience joy, just like Saturday, Friday, and Thursday. Monday too. Oh, and also Tuesday and Wednesday. When you distinguish each moment as a choice to do something meaningful, you learn to place importance on all of your time. You learn that you'll never waste a Sunday on anxiety, worry, or stress again.

The Importance of Summer

As a school administrator, summertime can serve as a well-deserved break from the grind of the school year. It can also serve as a time to build a routine of productivity. Each year, I print a summer checklist just as school is ending in June. The checklist has the standard tasks that need to be completed each summer (class lists, schedules, information to teachers/parents, welcome back letters, building repairs and maintenance, etc.). While summer serves as a much more relaxed time during an otherwise slammed school year, it also serves as the perfect time to simply get things done.

In my building, the only twelve-month employees are our custodians, our head secretary, and me. The custodians spend the summer doing an amazing job of cleaning the school and getting it ready for the new school year. Our head secretary handles all student registrations, purchasing, and inventorying supplies as they come in during the summer. I typically work off of my summer list. Because I manage to be so productive during the school year (class schedules and class placements are often done before I finish the school year), I am able to take a relaxed approach to being productive during the summer. I work through my summer list without any of the daily fires that occur during the school year. It's nice to be able to sit completely focused on a single task and finish it without any disruptions.

> **SYSTEMS CHECK**
>
> What tasks can you complete uninterrupted during the quiet summer months that will help to take something off your plate during the busy months of the school year?

The Quicker Picker Upper

If you are familiar with the large green package of paper towels, you may know that Bounty is the "quicker picker upper." If you've seen the commercials, you know that Bounty is promoted as being more absorbent than all other paper towels. In this spirit, you can use the summer to become a quicker picker upper yourself. You have the chance to quickly and more efficiently handle all of your responsibilities and duties when no one else is around to add more to your plate. The summer can absorb more than any other time of year for you. Here are some tips and strategies for being super productive this summer.

Start with your summer list. Even with the relaxed pace of summer, the quiet and lack of immediate pressure can make it tough to get started. That's why, every June, I print out my summer task list. It's a comprehensive rundown of all the administrative duties—welcome letters, class lists, schedules, and more—that need to happen. Creating this yearly list is a productivity game changer. I can just glance at it and dive right in. I recommend making a digital version so you can easily tweak it each year. This summer, I'll add several hiring-related tasks. Get your own list together, and you'll find your summer suddenly becomes much more efficient.

Create and add dates to your calendar. I love to go into the year with all of our calendar dates decided. I spend a good amount of time during the summer outlining all of our dates for the year, ensuring that nothing overlaps, and giving everyone as much heads-up as I can on annual dates. Planning staff meetings, curriculum meetings, professional development, assemblies, student awards, field trips, PTA events, and anything else gives you a huge head start on the year. Add all of the dates to a shared digital calendar so that everyone is fully aware of when things are happening. Everyone will appreciate going in with a twenty-thousand-foot view of the school year.

Review data and plan accordingly. During the school year, finding time for in-depth data analysis feels like spinning plates. There's just too much going on. While I collaborate with our data team throughout the year, summer offers dedicated time to really dig in and focus. It's the perfect opportunity to thoughtfully analyze data, pinpoint areas needing intervention, and map out a detailed plan. Once you've identified trends and crafted your strategy, have your data team review it when they're back in the fall.

Explore new technology. Finding time during the school year to explore technology can be difficult. I'm one of those people that needs to practice and explore consistently in order to learn a new tech tool. The school year usually provides only sporadic times to explore. Summer provides a more consistent time frame. Connect with your district's tech team or tech facilitators to learn about the latest and greatest tech tools. Spend a week trying one or two out, and prepare a turnkey presentation to share with staff when they return for the new year.

Grant writing. There is a ton of money available to do some amazing things in your school. If you've never written a grant before, the summer serves as a perfect, no-pressure time to write your first. Research some grants that you think might be helpful to your school or teachers—hands-on science projects, a new set of phys ed equipment, or new technology for your school. Use AI to generate a basic outline of the grant process. Follow through on the specific guidelines from the grant, and write your proposal. If your district employs a grant writer, connect with them to learn about the process, collaborate to write, and receive feedback on your proposal. There's no better time to tackle grant writing than the summer.

Organize and declutter. If you are anything like me, you kind of throw everything around in your office during the school year. I usually spend the first couple of summer days decluttering my office—going through everything, filing what needs to be filed, and tossing what deserves to be tossed. As educators, we usually hold onto things twenty years too long. Try to minimize what you have in your office. Get rid of the printed copies that you have somewhere digitally. Throw away stuff that you'll never use again. Just try to get more organized so that your office can help you to reach a functional workflow. Remember, less is more. Be a quicker picker upper and get rid of those messes.

Summer provides the perfect opportunity to be a quicker picker upper. You can pick up all of those tasks that fell off of the table during the school year. You can be more efficient and productive with no one else around to disturb you. Use your time wisely. Relax, of course, but also get a head start on the school year. You are a Quicker Picker Upper!

Travel Size (or a Trial Period)

You're getting ready to go on a trip, so you head to your local big-box store or grocery store and head down that aisle that has all of the travel-size stuff. Deodorants, toothbrushes with little plastic hats, shampoo, conditioner, mini first aid kits, strawberry lip balm. This list could literally go on for nineteen more pages. Whenever I get ready to take a trip, I make it a priority to see what kind of travel-size stuff I can take and try out for a few days. I sort of love this aisle because it gives me a chance to try out a bunch of stuff I've never tried before.

We should also take this approach when working toward productivity. Trying something out for a few days to see if it works for us can be very beneficial. You can take a trial period for a week with one of the strategies and see if it works for you. If it doesn't, you can go back to your previous method or try another new strategy for another week. If it does work, you can adopt it wholesale. These tips can help as you try out different methods to find what works for you.

Summer trials. The summer provides a perfect opportunity to try out some new ideas without the pressure of the school year. You'll be able to mess with your inbox format, try several different options, and decide what format is more efficient for you. Less pressure. More time to play around and explore. Implement your experimentation in the summer months when you have more free time.

Explore with new tech tools. Did you just learn about the latest technology at a conference? Give yourself a week to try it out. See how you can utilize the tech tool in a variety of ways during a typical week. Putting a tech tool into practice is really the best way to determine its usefulness. You'll find out quickly whether the new tool is worth the effort and is something that you need to adopt full-time.

Utilize unique time frames. There are certain times during the school year where you are faced with unique and unusual schedules. In New Jersey, we refer to "No-School November," when the month seems we have more days off than on. In the week before Thanksgiving, for example, there are only two-and-a-half days of school. Try an A/B trial where you utilize one new email format on Monday and a different one on Tuesday. Spend Wednesday morning examining the pros and cons of both formats and determine whether either method should replace your current method. Other short weeks or time periods where your schedule is minimized can be a great time to explore and discover new ways to become more productive.

Delegate your trials. Chances are that others may have tried a productivity method you're interested in. Promote a productivity PD session where you introduce two automation strategies to staff and give them a week to implement either method. Meet again a week later to share and discuss what worked and what didn't. You'll find that your colleagues will be able to pinpoint the traps of each method while also determining the efficiency of the new routines.

Record your feedback, output, and comfort level. When you're trying out a new tool or strategy, consistent reflection is key. If you test something on Monday and don't revisit it until Wednesday, it's easy to lose those initial impressions. Make sure to jot down notes as you're going, and, when you're done with the trial, record your feedback and outcomes. Did the tool work? Did the strategy improve things? Most importantly, note how you felt—were you comfortable? Does it feel sustainable? Did you dislike the method even if it worked? All these details matter. Capture everything in your notebook to track your progress and make informed decisions about what works best for you.

The Best Twenty Dollars I Ever Spent

Distractions can really put a cramp on our productive lives. If you've ever sat down to get something done, but just can't focus, it can be a real bummer. You know exactly what you need to do, but every other thing makes its way into your mind, stopping you from getting it done. I have a simple fix that I think will help.

Twenty bucks. That's all I paid. As I sit here at the keyboard right now, it's working in the background, keeping me focused. I am able to dominate my day with intense focus because of a simple twenty-dollar gadget.

It came about a few years ago, when my daughter asked for and received a white noise machine for Christmas. It's a small device that plays more than forty different soundtracks including babbling brooks, running water, fuzz, birds, waves, frogs, drifting snow, and crickets. My daughter's favorite soundtrack was a steady rain that helped her to fall asleep.

It seemed like it might help me with my focus problem, so I decided to order one. It was the best twenty dollars I've ever spent. My go-to soundtrack is a consistent piano melody that allows me to get into a zone. Every time I sit to write in my home office, the piano tune plays, establishing a time to focus on writing. Since it worked so well at home, I decided to purchase a couple for school. One made its way into the cafeteria to provide some ambient background noise during lunches to help tame the crowds.

The other white noise machine is housed in our main office, where, during the winter months, we set it to play a crackling fireplace that somehow makes it seem warmer in the office. As the winter months turn to warmer weather, we play the simulated waves crashing at the beach, which sets a certain mood.

I have also used it in my own office to provide specific soundtracks for work. There's a second, different piano melody that I utilize whenever I'm writing a letter or communication with families. There's also a dull hum that I use when I'm working on the budget each year. Other favorites include a thunderstorm, steady rainfall, and the sound of the forest. It's nice to associate certain tasks with certain soundtracks. It puts you into the mindset of getting necessary work done.

It is the best twenty dollars I've ever spent. I suggest getting one for yourself to help you be more focused.

> **CONTROL PANEL CHECK: REMINDER EMAILS**
>
> If you are anything like me, you'll think of something that you need to do at the most inopportune times. Just about to lay down to go to bed? Of course, you will think of those three documents you need to search for in the morning. If you go to bed without doing anything about the thought, you might be up all night, or the thought might be completely gone in the morning. To get the thought out of my head, I have developed a simple tactic.
>
> I email myself a reminder. While I don't have my school email on my phone, I have another account set up just for this purpose. I send my school email account as basic a message as possible:
>
> *Search three documents*
>
> Now the email is right there in my inbox the next morning, and I have the simple reminder that I need to tackle this task. So next time, don't forget. Try emailing yourself instead.

Preflight Checklist for Routines and Rituals for Success

- ❏ What strategy from this chapter would you like to try?
- ❏ Why? (your true north)
- ❏ How? (your plan)
- ❏ When? (your timeline)

OUR FINAL APPROACH

It's time that we begin our final approach to unparalleled productivity. Going on autopilot certainly requires a commitment, but you've already picked up the book, so I'm not worried about your level of commitment. You are going to find that as you eliminate, delegate, and minimize, you will make time for the tasks and projects that are most meaningful. You'll have more time in your day, and you'll streamline all of your processes. Systems thinking will replace one-track thinking that keeps you in survival mode. Productivity is a mindset. Once you start thinking this way, you'll find that it transfers over to the rest of your life as well. You'll stop wasting time—unless, of course, you plan to waste time. Remember that, sometimes, it's a perfectly acceptable thing to do.

Your new approach will cause you to rethink everything. You'll wonder why you've done things a certain way for many years. You'll also find that those around you will continue to find better ways to do things. At the end of the school year, each of our classes is hosted by our parent-teacher organization at an off-site picnic. The off-site location is just across the street from our school, and during my time at the school, parents who were taking their children home early after the picnic always had to bring their child back to the school to sign them out. While going through the process this year, one of our main office staff asked why we had kids sign out in the building instead of just signing out off site. I had no good answer to the question, so we streamlined the process.

This is what you'll do. You will find things that, while not broken, certainly need to be reimagined. You will adjust your systems and make yourself and those around you more efficient. It's time for you to reimagine your life as a productive and innovative school leader. It's time to go on autopilot.

Going on autopilot isn't about creating the perfect schedule. It's about optimizing. It's about streamlining. Getting stuff done. But make sure it's meaningful stuff. Going on autopilot is about meeting your goals while still finding time for joy, both professionally and personally. It means experimenting to find the things that work for you. Not everything that I suggested in this book is going to work for you, and that's OK. Being on autopilot means trying out certain methods, tweaking them, and bringing them full circle to ensure your efficiency.

Seth Godin is a prolific writer, author, blogger, and podcast host. He was once asked during a guest appearance on the National Council of Teachers of English podcast *Why I Write* to describe his writing process. He challenged the premise of the question and explained that the writing process is irrelevant. His point was that all successful writers have any number of things that lead to their success, and if he shared his "process," it might limit how others approached their own process. Productivity works much the same way.

Productivity is in the eye of the beholder. What may be productive for me may not approach productive for you. A strategy that works wonders for me may not work at all for you. This book has provided many strategies that you may find helpful. You may also already have strategies that work for you. I'm encouraging you to find your own way. Try things. Experiment. Find the methods that work for you, and eliminate those that do not. Share the ideas with others. Talk about what makes you efficient, and find out what strategies others use. There is no one way toward productivity. It's a journey, and there are many stops and starts along the way.

So, as you begin your new journey, it's important that you consider your flight plan.

DESIGNING YOUR FLIGHT PLAN

You've now read through the strategies and, hopefully, you have a better idea of how you are going to approach your day. While I want everyone who reads this book to become more productive and automated in some way, I also want to present you with the plan to become a *pro*(ductivity) *pro*(fessional). By becoming a pro pro, you will commit yourself to organization, output, and automation.

Before every flight, the pilot of an aircraft reviews the flight plan. It includes information about the trip: an intended flight path, departure and arrival times, an estimated time of the flight, and info on the plane, pilot, and passengers on board. To finish out this book, you are going to focus on your FLIGHT plan. This plan will help you to become a pro pro who can streamline for efficiency, make time for the meaningful, and get the most out of your day. The FLIGHT plan will outline six steps that will help you optimize your day to become more automated and productive. The six steps follow below:

- Find your pain points.
- List your wins.
- Implement systems.

- Give it a shot.
- Habit stack your day.
- Time block your day.

Let's outline how each of these next steps can help you to become a pro pro. You can write in the book or use the FLIGHT plan template found on the *Autopilot* website. (Look for a link at the end of the book!)

Find your pain points. We spent some time earlier in the book identifying pain points. You can go back to that section, or you can now think clearly about where you might be currently struggling. Think about what's holding you back. Has email become a black hole of time for you? Are you tied up by the requests and demands of others? Do you struggle with the basics? Have you not figured out how to help yourself? Finding the areas that are causing the most pain will allow you to address them directly. If you know what's wrong, you can easily fix it. For our final FLIGHT plan, I want you to list your three biggest pain points. The rest of our plan will help to map our solutions to these three areas. Here are some possible pain points:

- email taking up too much time
- lack of efficiency with schedule
- can't say no
- too much paperwork or administrivia

Now that you know exactly what needs to be addressed, let's find out some other areas where you may already be successful.

List your wins. We've been over this before, but if you've already picked up this book, you may be someone who is already productive and looking for more ways to streamline your day. Let's look at some of the areas that have already been fruitful, and see if we can glean anything from them. If you have already experienced productivity and automation wins, you are well on your way to being more successful by making a few tweaks to the above-listed pain points.

Your success in the below areas may guide us in our next steps. List your three biggest automation or productivity wins. Your possible wins may include the following:

- established routine communication with families
- tamed the email beast
- utilized technology to minimize busywork

Now that we can look at some of your positive gains, we can start to formulate our plan.

Implement systems. The key to success in becoming a pro pro is not to implement one or two of the strategies from this book or other hacks that you find online. The key is being able to tackle your pain points from a systems perspective. You need to address your problems head-on in a systematic way that actually eliminates the problems rather than finding makeshift solutions. Your systems approach may include implementing a new plan for email (including time blocks, structural changes to your inbox, and a new philosophical approach). You might tackle your workload issue with a systems approach to customer support tickets to ensure that nothing is lost or forgotten. You may wish to address the following systems:

- communication
- resource management or deployment
- time management
- technology integration

Let's think about three systems that you will address as you move forward.

Now that you have an overarching idea of how to address systems that will impact your day, let's get to some specifics.

Give it a shot. When my daughter was very young (think preschool age), she would encourage me and my wife (and even herself) to try new things by saying, "Give it a shot!" The saying became a way of motivating our family to try things and not worry about the outcome.

I want to provide the same sentiment here. Regardless of what you've identified as your pain points, and what systems thinking you are going to put in place to go on autopilot, I want you to commit to three specific tasks or items that you will try to put in place to become more automated or productive. Even if the three things that you try don't work out for you, you just might learn something from the implementation practice. I've recently begun coaching my son's hockey teams and added another saying that I think applies here: We don't win or lose, we win or learn. By trying something out, you may end up with a huge win for yourself, or you may learn from the implementation.

Give it a shot. List three specific strategies or ideas you will try out. You may wish to try these out:

- use a management app (like Trello or Todoist) to manage tasks, delegate, and keep track of progress
- streamline communication by introducing Slack, reducing the number of emails, and improving response time
- automate family communications using Smore newsletters
- efficiently use Google Drive for the storage, retrieval, and sharing of documents

Now that we have some things to try, we need to apply what we've learned from the shot you've given.

Habit block your day. We know what we need to do to be successful at this point. We just have to put those plans into place. It's time now to start creating habits out of our plans that will help us find success. There is debate about how long it takes to create a new habit. If you've ever tried to replace a bad habit with a good one, it can take a while. Some people will form a new habit in less than a month. Some will take three to six months. Building habitual routines into your day is going to help you stick to your FLIGHT plan and become a pro pro. Let's take a few moments to list some of the habits that you'll add to your daily or weekly schedule:

- a goal-setting morning routine
- an end-of-day shutdown, reflection, and tidying time
- a closed door or cave time when you actually get stuff done
- office hours when you can meet and communicate with colleagues

Now that we have some standard practices built into our day, we need to address one more area that's going to help us be successful.

Time block your schedule. The pièce de résistance to your new approach to automation and productivity is going to be to time block your schedule. This means that you will dedicate specific time periods each day to specific tasks and, at all costs, attempt to stick to those time blocks. If you give yourself forty-five minutes to check and respond to emails, don't let it take an hour and a half. Building a routine of time blocking your schedule will keep you to a strict regimen of accomplishing your goals. Time blocking allows you to focus on what needs to be addressed, while minimizing other distractions and ensuring that priority tasks get done first. Here are some suggested time blocks to build into your day:

- morning planning and review (thirty minutes)
- classroom visits and walk-throughs (thirty-minute blocks)
- administrative minutiae minutes (twenty-to-thirty-minute blocks)
- open office hours (thirty-minute blocks)

You now have your FLIGHT plan ready, and you can move forward on your journey to productivity!

EARN YOUR PRODUCTIVITY WINGS

I remember my first time on an airplane. I was seven years old and flying to Florida. The reason I remember this is because, as I was exiting the plane, the pilot handed me my own set of Eastern Airlines wings like the ones he was wearing. Granted they were a cheap, plastic version of the pilot's wings, but to seven-year-old me, they represented a great accomplishment. I was damn proud of those wings.

Now that you have completed your FLIGHT plan for going on autopilot, I want to provide the opportunity for you to earn your productivity wings. You've learned a great deal about how you can be more successful by automating, delegating, and thinking critically about how you use your time.

I'm sure you've had enough of that overwhelming feeling, like you aren't quite accomplishing what you should be, or you're tired of taking work home with you that doesn't get done during the day. You need to feel successful. You need to make more free time in your schedule so that you can better support students and teachers. Don't keep reinventing the wheel. Don't stress and worry about all of the menial tasks. Leave more room for the fun stuff and build a more positive and productive school culture.

The power of committing to the autopilot mindset is connection. Once you embrace the autopilot mindset, you will unlock a deeper connection with your work, your colleagues, and yourself. By freeing your mental space and your schedule, you'll create room for the kind of meaningful interactions that fuel a positive school culture. Imagine the impact of being present, energized, and ready to collaborate, rather than constantly feeling overwhelmed and behind.

Your FLIGHT plan is your ticket to earning your productivity wings right now. Not cheap plastic ones, but the real deal—the kind that signify mastery, leadership, and a genuine transformation in how you approach your role. By implementing your FLIGHT plan and consistently working toward autopilot, you are not just improving your life but setting an example for your entire school community. Show them what it means to be efficient, focused, and fulfilled. Show everyone how you have soared to new heights.

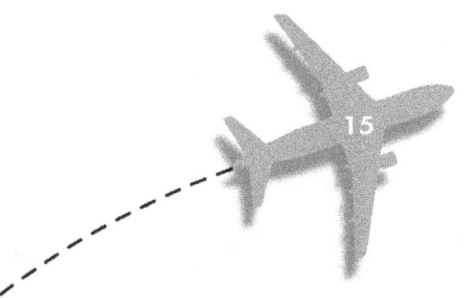

A FINAL MESSAGE FROM OUR CAPTAIN

This is your captain speaking with final instructions as we approach our destination.

Please adjust your seats to their upright position and prepare to make this your own journey.

I hope you have enjoyed our trip to unparalleled productivity. Please know that the journey doesn't end here. In fact, it's just beginning, and now you're in the pilot's seat.

You get to make the decisions. You get to decide how to make it easier, more efficient, less stressful, and streamlined. You're the captain now.

Continue to soar, continue to inspire, and continue to lead with purpose.

Thank you for choosing Autopilot as your guide on this journey.

BEYOND AUTOPILOT

The final bell echoes, signaling the end of another school day. As students rush out, their laughter fades into the distance. But for you, the work never truly ends.

The journey to peak productivity is ongoing; it's about embracing challenges and seeking out opportunities for growth.

Autopilot has provided the road map for streamlining your workflow and maximizing your impact. But remember, this is just the beginning.

As I sat in the theater with my children at the latest Marvel movie waiting for the credits to roll, anticipating what was coming, I was inspired to write this section. As another scene sprang to life on the screen, I was inspired to discover what comes next.

In the spirit of the Marvel movies that we all love, consider this your postcredits scene, a glimpse into the future with autopilot. Stay curious. Give it a shot, keep experimenting, and never stop striving for your best.

The future of education depends on leaders like you who are willing to go above and beyond.

The autopilot journey continues . . .

Start your journey beyond autopilot with this QR code.

Find more autopilot resources, connections, videos, and ideas!

ACKNOWLEDGMENTS

I'd like to thank Megan, Meredith, Olivia, and Malcolm for allowing me to continue to pursue writing and for their love and support, always.

I'd like to thank the following people who have helped me along my own productivity journey: Max Achtau, Jay Billy, Trevor Bryan, Mike Bryce, Barb Carmignani, Tony Cattani, Cara Flodmand, Alex Handzus, Tania Katan, Christine Keelan, Shaun Laurito, Liz Lillo, Sydney Matejik, James Sterenczak, and Kara Stern. Each of you has helped me in one way or another, whether it was sharing an idea, sharing a space, talking through what shouldn't be done or how it could be done, lending a helpful hand, keeping me afloat, providing support, or putting an idea in my head that just wouldn't go away. You've all done more than you realize.

#Gratitude

ABOUT RICH CZYZ

Rich Czyz (pronounced "Chiz") is the proud principal of Yardville Elementary School and cofounder of fouroclockfaculty.com. He is a passionate writer and has authored four books: *The Four O'Clock Faculty*, *The SECRET SAUCE*, *ROGUE Leader*, and *Autopilot*. Rich is dedicated to creating productive environments and engaging all stakeholders in meaningful and relevant learning opportunities.

Rich is available for consulting opportunities, speaking engagements, presentations, professional development training, speeches, and keynote addresses on a wide range of relevant education topics. Please email 4oclockfaculty@gmail.com for more information.

MORE FROM

Since 2012, DBCI has published books that inspire and equip educators to be their best. For more information on our titles or to purchase bulk orders for your school, district, or book study, visit DaveBurgessConsulting.com/DBCIbooks.

The *Like a PIRATE*™ Series

Teach Like a PIRATE by Dave Burgess

Balance Like a PIRATE by Jessica Cabeen, Jessica Johnson, and Sarah Johnson

eXPlore Like a PIRATE by Michael Matera

Learn Like a PIRATE by Paul Solarz

Plan Like a PIRATE by Dawn M. Harris

Play Like a PIRATE by Quinn Rollins

Run Like a PIRATE by Adam Welcome

Tech Like a PIRATE by Matt Miller

The *Lead Like a PIRATE*™ Series

Lead Like a PIRATE by Shelley Burgess and Beth Houf

Lead Beyond Your Title by Nili Bartley

Lead with Appreciation by Amber Teamann and Melinda Miller

Lead with Collaboration by Allyson Apsey and Jessica Gomez

Lead with Culture by Jay Billy

Lead with Instructional Rounds by Vicki Wilson

Lead with Literacy by Mandy Ellis

She Leads by Dr. Rachael George and Majalise W. Tolan

The EduProtocol Field Guide Series

Deploying EduProtocols by Kim Voge, with Jon Corippo and Marlena Hebern

The EduProtocol Field Guide by Marlena Hebern and Jon Corippo

The EduProtocol Field Guide Book 2 by Marlena Hebern and Jon Corippo

The EduProtocol Field Guide ELA Edition by Jacob Carr

The EduProtocol Field Guide Math Edition by Lisa Nowakowski and Jeremiah Ruesch

The EduProtocol Field Guide Primary Edition by Benjamin Cogswell and Jennifer Dean

The EduProtocol Field Guide Social Studies Edition by Dr. Scott M. Petri and Adam Moler

Leadership & School Culture

Be 1% Better by Ron Clark

Be THAT Teacher by Dwayne Reed

Beyond the Surface of Restorative Practices by Marisol Rerucha

Change the Narrative by Henry J. Turner and Kathy Lopes

Choosing to See by Pamela Seda and Kyndall Brown

Culturize by Jimmy Casas

Discipline Win by Andy Jacks

Educate Me! by Dr. Shree Walker with Michael D. Ison

Escaping the School Leader's Dunk Tank by Rebecca Coda and Rick Jetter

Fight Song by Kim Bearden

From Teacher to Leader by Starr Sackstein

MORE FROM DAVE BURGESS CONSULTING, INC.

If the Dance Floor Is Empty, Change the Song by Joe Clark

The Innovator's Mindset by George Couros

It's OK to Say "They" by Christy Whittlesey

Kids Deserve It! by Todd Nesloney and Adam Welcome

Leading the Whole Teacher by Allyson Apsey

Let Them Speak by Rebecca Coda and Rick Jetter

The Limitless School by Abe Hege and Adam Dovico

Live Your Excellence by Jimmy Casas

Next-Level Teaching by Jonathan Alsheimer

The Pepper Effect by Sean Gaillard

Principaled by Kate Barker, Kourtney Ferrua, and Rachael George

The Principled Principal by Jeffrey Zoul and Anthony McConnell

Relentless by Hamish Brewer

The Secret Solution by Todd Whitaker, Sam Miller, and Ryan Donlan

Start. Right. Now. by Todd Whitaker, Jeffrey Zoul, and Jimmy Casas

Stop. Right. Now. by Jimmy Casas and Jeffrey Zoul

Teach Your Class Off by CJ Reynolds

Teachers Deserve It by Rae Hughart and Adam Welcome

They Call Me "Mr. De" by Frank DeAngelis

Thrive Through the Five by Jill M. Siler

Unmapped Potential by Julie Hasson and Missy Lennard

When Kids Lead by Todd Nesloney and Adam Dovico

Word Shift by Joy Kirr

Your School Rocks by Ryan McLane and Eric Lowe

Technology & Tools

50 Things to Go Further with Google Classroom by Alice Keeler and Libbi Miller

50 Things You Can Do with Google Classroom by Alice Keeler and Libbi Miller

50 Ways to Engage Students with Google Apps by Alice Keeler and Heather Lyon

140 Twitter Tips for Educators by Brad Currie, Billy Krakower, and Scott Rocco

AI Optimism by Becky Keene

Block Breaker by Brian Aspinall

Building Blocks for Tiny Techies by Jamila "Mia" Leonard

Code Breaker by Brian Aspinall

The Complete EdTech Coach by Katherine Goyette and Adam Juarez

Control Alt Achieve by Eric Curts

The Esports Education Playbook by Chris Aviles, Steve Isaacs, Christine Lion-Bailey, and Jesse Lubinsky

Google Apps for Littles by Christine Pinto and Alice Keeler

Master the Media by Julie Smith

Raising Digital Leaders by Jennifer Casa-Todd

Reality Bytes by Christine Lion-Bailey, Jesse Lubinsky, and Micah Shippee, PhD

Sail the 7 Cs with Microsoft Education by Becky Keene and Kathi Kersznowski

Shake Up Learning by Kasey Bell

Social LEADia by Jennifer Casa-Todd

Stepping Up to Google Classroom by Alice Keeler and Kimberly Mattina

Teaching Math with Google Apps by Alice Keeler and Diana Herrington

Teaching with Google Jamboard by Alice Keeler and Kimberly Mattina

Teachingland by Amanda Fox and Mary Ellen Weeks

Teaching Methods & Materials

All 4s and 5s by Andrew Sharos

MORE FROM DAVE BURGESS CONSULTING, INC.

Boredom Busters by Katie Powell

Building Strong Writers by Christina Schneider

The Classroom Chef by John Stevens and Matt Vaudrey

The Collaborative Classroom by Trevor Muir

Copyrighteous by Diana Gill

CREATE by Bethany J. Petty

Ditch That Homework by Matt Miller and Alice Keeler

Ditch That Textbook by Matt Miller

Don't Ditch That Tech by Matt Miller, Nate Ridgway, and Angelia Ridgway

EDrenaline Rush by John Meehan

Educated by Design by Michael Cohen, The Tech Rabbi

Empowered to Choose: A Practical Guide to Personalized Learning by Andrew Easton

Expedition Science by Becky Schnekser

Frustration Busters by Katie Powell

Fully Engaged by Michael Matera and John Meehan

Game On? Brain On! by Lindsay Portnoy, PhD

Guided Math AMPED by Reagan Tunstall

Happy & Resilient by Roni Habib

Innovating Play by Jessica LaBar-Twomy and Christine Pinto

Instant Relevance by Denis Sheeran

Instructional Coaching Connection by Nathan Lang-Raad

Keeping the Wonder by Jenna Copper, Ashley Bible, Abby Gross, and Staci Lamb

LAUNCH by John Spencer and A.J. Juliani

Learning in the Zone by Dr. Sonny Magana

Less Talk, More Action by Allyson Apsey and Emily Freeland

Lights, Cameras, TEACH! by Kevin J. Butler

Make Learning MAGICAL by Tisha Richmond

Pass the Baton by Kathryn Finch and Theresa Hoover
Project-Based Learning Anywhere by Lori Elliott
Pure Genius by Don Wettrick
The Revolution by Darren Ellwein and Derek McCoy
The Science Box by Kim Adsit and Adam Peterson
Shift This! by Joy Kirr
Skyrocket Your Teacher Coaching by Michael Cary Sonbert
Spark Learning by Ramsey Musallam
Sparks in the Dark by Travis Crowder and Todd Nesloney
Table Talk Math by John Stevens
Teachables by Cheryl Abla and Lisa Maxfield
Unpack Your Impact by Naomi O'Brien and LaNesha Tabb
The Wild Card by Hope and Wade King
Writefully Empowered by Jacob Chastain
The Writing on the Classroom Wall by Steve Wyborney
You Are Poetry by Mike Johnston
You'll Never Guess What I'm Saying by Naomi O'Brien
You'll Never Guess What I'm Thinking About by Naomi O'Brien

Inspiration, Professional Growth & Personal Development

Be REAL by Tara Martin
Be the One for Kids by Ryan Sheehy
The Coach ADVenture by Amy Illingworth
Creatively Productive by Lisa Johnson
The Ed Branding Book by Dr. Renae Bryant and Lynette White
Educational Eye Exam by Alicia Ray
The EduNinja Mindset by Jennifer Burdis
Empower Our Girls by Lynmara Colón and Adam Welcome
Finding Lifelines by Andrew Grieve and Andrew Sharos

The Four O'Clock Faculty by Rich Czyz

How Much Water Do We Have? by Pete and Kris Nunweiler

P Is for Pirate by Dave and Shelley Burgess

A Passion for Kindness by Tamara Letter

The Path to Serendipity by Allyson Apsey

PheMOMenal Teacher by Annick Rauch

Recipes for Resilience by Robert A. Martinez

Rogue Leader by Rich Czyz

Sanctuaries by Dan Tricarico

Saving Sycamore by Molly B. Hudgens

The Secret Sauce by Rich Czyz

Shattering the Perfect Teacher Myth by Aaron Hogan

Stories from Webb by Todd Nesloney

Talk to Me by Kim Bearden

Teach Better by Chad Ostrowski, Tiffany Ott, Rae Hughart, and Jeff Gargas

Teach Me, Teacher by Jacob Chastain

Teach, Play, Learn! by Adam Peterson

The Teachers of Oz by Herbie Raad and Nathan Lang-Raad

Teaching Is a Tattoo by Mike Johnston

Teaching the Ms. Abbott Way by Joyce Stephens Abbott

TeamMakers by Laura Robb and Evan Robb

Through the Lens of Serendipity by Allyson Apsey

Write Here and Now by Dan Tricarico

The Zen Teacher by Dan Tricarico

Children's Books

The Adventures of Little Mickey by Mickey Smith Jr.

Alpert by LaNesha Tabb

Alpert & Friends by LaNesha Tabb

Beyond Us by Aaron Polansky

Cannonball In by Tara Martin

Dolphins in Trees by Aaron Polansky

Dragon Smart by Tisha and Tommy Richmond

I Can Achieve Anything by MoNique Waters

I Want to Be a Lot by Ashley Savage

The Magic of Wonder by Jenna Copper, Ashley Bible, Abby Gross, and Staci Lamb

Micah's Big Question by Naomi O'Brien

The Princes of Serendip by Allyson Apsey

Ride with Emilio by Richard Nares

A Teacher's Top Secret Confidential by LaNesha Tabb

A Teacher's Top Secret: Mission Accomplished by LaNesha Tabb

The Wild Card Kids by Hope and Wade King

Zom-Be a Design Thinker by Amanda Fox

www.ingramcontent.com/pod-product-compliance
Lightning Source LLC
Chambersburg PA
CBHW050527170426
43201CB00013B/2111